LIVING WITH CIVILISATIONS

REFLECTIONS ON SOUTHEAST ASIA'S LOCAL AND NATIONAL CULTURES

IPS-Nathan Lecture Series

Print ISSN: 2630-4996
Online ISSN: 2630-5003

Published

Vol. 12: *Living with Civilisations: Reflections on Southeast Asia's Local and National Cultures*
by Wang Gungwu

Vol. 11: *Stewardship of the Singapore Media: Staying the Course*
by Patrick Daniel

Vol. 10: *Singapore and Multilateral Governance: Securing Our Future*
by Noeleen Heyzer

Vol. 9: *The Singapore Synthesis: Innovation, Inclusion, Inspiration*
by Ravi Menon

Vol. 8: *Gender Equality: The Time Has Come*
by Corinna Lim

Vol. 7: *World in Transition: Singapore's Future*
by Chan Heng Chee

Vol. 6: *The Idea of Singapore: Smallness Unconstrained*
by Tan Tai Yong

Vol. 5: *Seeking a Better Urban Future*
by Cheong Koon Hean

Vol. 4: *Can Singapore Fall?: Making the Future for Singapore*
by Lim Siong Guan

Vol. 3: *The Challenges of Governance in a Complex World*
by Peter Ho

More information on this series can also be found at https://www.worldscientific.com/series/ipsnls

IPS-NATHAN LECTURES

LIVING WITH CIVILISATIONS

REFLECTIONS ON SOUTHEAST ASIA'S LOCAL AND NATIONAL CULTURES

WANG GUNGWU

Published by

World Scientific Publishing Co. Pte. Ltd.
5 Toh Tuck Link, Singapore 596224
USA office: 27 Warren Street, Suite 401-402, Hackensack, NJ 07601
UK office: 57 Shelton Street, Covent Garden, London WC2H 9HE

National Library Board, Singapore Cataloguing in Publication Data
Name(s): Wang, Gungwu. | Institute of Policy Studies (Singapore)
Title: Living with civilisations : reflections on Southeast Asia's local and national cultures / Wang Gungwu.
Other Title(s): IPS-Nathan Lecture series.
Description: Singapore : World Scientific Publishing Co. Pte. Ltd., [2023]
Identifier(s): ISBN 978-981-12-8484-7 (hardcover) | ISBN 978-981-12-8502-8 (paperback) |
  ISBN 978-981-12-8485-4 (ebook for institutions) |
  ISBN 978-981-12-8486-1 (ebook for individuals)
Subject(s): LCSH: Southeast Asia--Civilization. | Southeast Asia--Civilization--Foreign influences. | Singapore--Civilization. | Singapore--Civilization--Foreign influences.
Classification: DDC 959--dc23

British Library Cataloguing-in-Publication Data
A catalogue record for this book is available from the British Library.

Copyright © 2023 by Wang Gungwu & Institute of Policy Studies, National University of Singapore

All rights reserved.

For any available supplementary material, please visit
https://www.worldscientific.com/worldscibooks/10.1142/13638#t=suppl

Desk Editor: Kura Sunaina

Typeset by Stallion Press
Email: enquiries@stallionpress.com

THE S R NATHAN FELLOWSHIP FOR THE STUDY OF SINGAPORE

AND THE IPS-NATHAN LECTURE SERIES

The S R Nathan Fellowship for the Study of Singapore was established by the Institute of Policy Studies (IPS) in 2013 to support research on public policy and governance issues. With the generous contributions of individual and corporate donors, and a matching government grant, IPS raised around S$5.9 million to endow the Fellowship.

Each S R Nathan Fellow, appointed under the Fellowship, delivers a series of IPS-Nathan Lectures during his or her term. These public lectures aim to promote public understanding and discourse on issues of critical national interest.

The Fellowship is named after Singapore's sixth and longest-serving President, the late S R Nathan, in recognition of his lifetime of service to Singapore.

CONTENTS

Foreword	ix
About the Moderators	xiii
About the Illustrator	xiv

Lecture I — Cultures and Civilisations — 1
   Question-and-Answer Session — 27
   Moderated by Professor Kwok Kian Woon

Lecture II — Opening to the Global Maritime — 41
   Question-and-Answer Session — 69
   Moderated by Dr Norshahril Saat

Lecture III — Enlightened Modern — 85
   Question-and-Answer Session — 113
   Moderated by Professor Elaine Ho

Lecture IV — Living Civilisations and National Cultures — 125
   Question-and-Answer Session — 151
   Moderated by Mr Bilahari Kausikan

Afterword — 165
Selected Bibliography — 169
Index — 193

FOREWORD

I

When Institute of Policy Studies Director Janadas Devan asked me to be the 12th S R Nathan Fellow, I was taken by surprise. I had been following the series of lectures given by previous Fellows and was impressed by how much each of the Fellows knew about Singapore's extraordinary story. They had lived through the crucial years of Singapore's growth to become the city-state that it is today. Each of them had engaged in affairs of governance and had been chosen to show what had to be done to build a modern nation.

I did not have those qualities. However, what Janadas might have known was that there was a Singapore heart within my home. My late wife Margaret had come from Shanghai as a young girl. She lived through the Japanese Occupation and studied at the Methodist Girls' School before joining the University of Malaya in 1950, a year after I did. For 18 years, her life was tied to Singapore. Although she became a wanderer's wife for the next 36 years, she never lost her deep affection for the city. She had followed its aspirations with intense interest, made sure that we visited Singapore regularly and kept in touch with our friends so that our long-distance view of the city-state would not be too far wrong. When Chan Heng Chee invited me to the Institute of Southeast Asian Studies (now known as ISEAS-Yusof Ishak Institute) on hearing of my retirement from Hong Kong University, Margaret encouraged me to accept. My *merantau* days were over and we made a new home. The 25 years I shared with Margaret here were happy and memorable years.

That, of course, does not qualify me to talk about Singapore. I am a historian and Tan Tai Yong had already fulfilled S R Nathan's wishes by providing a magisterial account of Singapore's history. Janadas understood that I can add nothing to that. So he gave me room to think beyond the horizon as long as Singapore was a part of what I had to say.

I went back to my memories of S R Nathan when we were students together in 1952 to 1954 and fellow members of the University Socialist Club. That was the time when we were learning about Southeast Asia as a strategic region. After graduation, our paths diverged. I did not see him again until I came in 1996 and he returned after being Singapore's ambassador to the United States (US). We were still engaged in thinking about our region and, unexpectedly, found ourselves in the business of running "think-tanks" in Singapore. As chairman of the Institute of East Asian Political Economy, I met him in his capacity as the first director of the Institute of Defence and Security Studies. After he was elected President of the Republic, he remained deeply concerned about our region as an enlarged ASEAN, and Singapore in Southeast Asia was our common interest.

Recalling our meeting took me back to my first impressions of Singapore as an undergraduate on the Bukit Timah Campus: these were centred on *Ujong Tanah* at the foot of the Malay Peninsula where people of *merantau* origins had settled. I shared my memories with Janadas and he agreed that they should help me find my way to give the lectures as S R Nathan Fellow.

II

During my first years of school, it was taken for granted that what I learnt represented British imperial culture at the peak of modern post-Enlightenment civilisation. In contrast, what my parents taught me at home came from ancient values already partly discarded in China. Adding another dimension to my education, I recall family conversations about China modernising in order to save the country from becoming colonised by a Japan that had set out to become a modern national empire.

I thus faced a huge knowledge gap between school and home every day and it became something I could not ignore. At the end of World War II, as a university student, I tried to understand what that meant and made efforts to fill the gap. There were moments of hope when Western imperialism retreated and a global institution was established that treated all nations as equals. But it soon became obvious that wealth and power as the measure of progress continued to determine who was civilised.

What saved me from cynicism was my growing awareness of Southeast Asia as a distinct region between India and China. A generation of scholars within and outside the region had discovered the linkages between local cultures and ancient Indic, Sinic and Islamic civilisations. Historians who focused on the cultural continuities noted how that helped the region deal with European national empires. They also saw the proud bearers of ancient civilisations selectively modernising in order to preserve their respective heritage. That helped me understand what different nations in our region were each doing to mould their multicultural societies into distinct identities.

However, the dominant discourse in global affairs was framed in terms of a single modern civilisation divided by two roads to wealth and power. When that represented by the Soviet Union ended in failure, the US became the sole superpower in a unipolar world. Thereafter, any country seen as challenging US supremacy was portrayed as a threat to the world order and even to civilisation itself.

The Chinese people had set out to modernise and restore pride in their civilisation and their two revolutions inevitably led them to the pursuit of wealth and power. Although they might have been content with a secure place in a multipolar world, their success was seen as ominous. As a result, the US and its allies decided to portray China as a threat to the unipolar world.

This set of lectures suggests that the study of local cultures and borderless civilisations can provide a different calculus of conflict and co-existence. Adding social, moral and spiritual heritage to the quest for modern development could check the obsessive concerns with poles of imperial power. Such a study would require that our multi-civilisational world be re-framed to demonstrate respect for the new identities that are being shaped by several civilisations. The fact that the peoples of Southeast Asia had long benefitted from that experience and continue to do so gives us hope. And when I saw how Singapore at its centre has successfully drawn on the region's multi-civilisational past to build a new city-nation, that led me to examine the phenomenon here.

III

I have already mentioned how grateful I am to Janadas Devan and the S R Nathan Fellowship Committee for inviting me and giving me the freedom to develop my ideas about the place of our region in world history. I wish also to thank my moderators, Kwok Kian Woon, Norshahril Saat, Elaine Ho and Bilahari Kausikan for skilfully guiding my audience to question me further about what I said. Most of all, a big thank you to associate director Liang Kaixin and my research assistant Latasha Seow Song-En who helped so vitally to make the lectures publishable.

Finally, many scholars and thinkers have, in one way or another over several decades, helped me with ideas about cultures and civilisations. I had problems mentioning all their writings here. In the end, I settled on providing a list of the books that had strongly influenced my thinking. For readers who wish to learn more about the turning points in the modern discourse, they will find relevant articles in the bibliographies of the books I have listed. I owe their authors a debt that I have no way of repaying. However, where errors of fact and interpretation are found, those are entirely my responsibility.

Wang Gungwu
30 July 2023

ABOUT THE MODERATORS

Professor Kwok Kian Woon is Vice-Chancellor, University of the Arts Singapore. He has been conferred an Emeritus Professorship at Nanyang Technological University, where he had served as Professor of Sociology and in several pioneering roles, including as a founding member of the former School of Humanities and Social Sciences, Head of Sociology, Senate Chair, Associate Provost of Student Life and Associate Vice President (Wellbeing). His research areas include the study of social memory, mental health, the Chinese overseas and Asian modernity. His publications and public engagements have covered central themes, such as ethics and politics; history and memory; the nation state and civil society and culture, heritage and the arts.

Dr Norshahril Saat is a Senior Fellow at the ISEAS-Yusof Ishak Institute (formerly known as Institute of Southeast Asian Studies, Singapore). He is the Coordinator of the Regional Social and Cultural Studies (RSCS) programme. In June 2015, he was awarded his doctorate in International, Political and Strategic Studies by the Australian National University (ANU). He is the author of *The State, Ulama, and Islam in Malaysia and Indonesia* (Amsterdam University Press/ISEAS-Yusof Ishak Institute); *Tradition and Islamic Learning: Singapore Students in the Al-Azhar University* (ISEAS-Yusof Ishak Institute) and *Faith, Authority and the Malays: The Ulama in Contemporary Singapore* (Malay Heritage Foundation).

Professor Elaine Lynn-Ee Ho is the Provost Chair Professor at the Department of Geography and Senior Research Fellow at the Asia Research Institute (ARI), National University of Singapore. Her research explores the geographies of citizenship, currently focusing on multidirectional migration and diasporas, and on transnationalism, ageing and care. She is the author of *Citizens in Motion: Emigration, Immigration and Re-migration Across China's Borders* (Stanford University Press), which received the American Sociological Association's (ASA) award for "Best Book in Global and Transnational Sociology by an International Scholar" in 2019. She is the editor of the journal *Social and Cultural Geography* and serves on the editorial boards of geography, migration, area and citizenship studies journals.

Mr Bilahari Kausikan is currently the Chairman of the Middle East Institute, an autonomous institute of the National University of Singapore. He has spent his entire career in the Ministry of Foreign Affairs. During his 37 years in the ministry, he served in a variety of appointments at home and abroad, including as Ambassador to the Russian Federation, Permanent Representative to the United Nations in New York and as the Permanent Secretary to the Ministry. Raffles Institution, the University of Singapore and Columbia University in New York all attempted to educate him.

ABOUT THE ILLUSTRATOR

Esther Goh is an illustrator and art director who works with brands across advertising, fashion, publishing and technology. Her illustrations have been recognised by D&AD, Cannes Design Lions, The One Show and Society of Illustrators, to name a few. In 2018, she was one of the Young Guns finalists, and in 2019, she was selected for the Generation T List by Asia Tatler.

Lecture I
CULTURES AND CIVILISATIONS

LECTURE I

The S R Nathan Fellowship has given me the chance to pursue my thoughts about Singapore as a new nation and share them with you. Those who gave lectures before me include friends who have a deep and intimate knowledge of public policy and governance. I do not have that knowledge and can only claim to be the oldest person to have been given the privilege. I did have a worm's-eye view of Singapore as a colony when Mr Nathan and I were students staying at the Dunearn Road Hostels.[1] We later briefly served the state when it was self-governing. There, I studied Singapore's place as the 12th state of the new Federation of Malaysia. Also, during the brief period when it was in the federation, I served on a committee to examine the city-state's contribution to the country's higher education.

After the separation, and until I came to work in Singapore in 1996, my associations with Singapore were desultory. They were a mixed set of experiences with everything about the Republic seen from outside and from afar. What was constantly in the news was the fact that this small state was in the middle of a newly defined region between two oceans. Most of the

---

[1] Dunearn Road Hostels were the student accommodation of the University of Malaya.

people were descended from immigrants from other countries who chose to settle here. Its leaders were nevertheless determined to create a national identity by incorporating parts of the several distinct cultures represented by its peoples.

The global city was determined to overcome its reputation as a cultural desert. It was committed to being part of modern civilisation while large sections of its population hoped to retain the cultural heritage of their ancestors. Many were conscious that their heritage came from ancient civilisations and that the three most prominent — the Indic, the Sinic and the Islamic — were living civilisations seeking to modernise. Together with their neighbours, Singapore was also reshaping a national culture within borders that had only recently been drawn.

This was something I found fascinating and I was curious what this really meant for the country. For decades, I had romanticised Singapore-in-Malaya as a colourful tapestry of local living and also a thick carpet that was woven with different strands of world history. There were moments when I had to stop painting pretty pictures of multicultural promise, for example, following the 13 May 1969 riots in Kuala Lumpur when the situation looked precarious. I had a personal perspective on racial and religious tensions, having been through the Maria Hertogh killings here. Also, I had briefly served on the committee set up to investigate the 1964 race riots in Singapore. How can a new nation be built with such explosive ingredients?

As a student of history, I was doing research on Chinese history, but I also had an interest in the overseas Chinese. These were the *huaqiao* in the Nanyang, an earlier name equated with the region called Southeast Asia. At the heart of that problem, beyond race and religion, were political issues of Chinese and local nationalisms intertwined with imperial capitalism and anti-colonial socialism.

I was losing my political innocence as I was studying more history and encountering ancient and modern civilisations. Before long, I saw the connection between local cultures and the external influences that came to shape and empower them. What was more, these influences often had deep roots, depending on when the peoples first came to the region, and how dynamic and powerful the neighbouring civilisations were.

The records and artefacts show that both the mainland and maritime peoples of our region did not produce their own civilisations. Instead, they chose what they wanted from those they were in contact with — all of them ancient civilisations that have survived to the present day.

There was the Indic civilisation from the Indian subcontinent. There was the Sinic civilisation in China coming from overland as well as from the South China Sea. And further west, there was the Mediterranean civilisation from across the Indian Ocean. This civilisation was later identified with a monotheistic faith that produced a profound division, branching into the Islamic and Christian faiths. The Arabic-based Islamic merchants reached our region early while the European crusaders and trading companies arrived only after the 16th century.

Major changes followed after the 18th century when the Age of Enlightenment in Europe led the world to the idea of *modern* civilisation. A new Singapore emerged out of the imperialist rivalries that mapped a region at the end of World War II, which the British called Southeast Asia. That region became one in which new nations were built and local cultures were being shaped into national cultures.

In the past 70 years, many efforts have been made to trace the origins of this region that did not have a name. The search for origins has been an intriguing adventure and we know a great deal more about our region today. But we are still trying to find meaning in the way our images of the past relate to present realities. Having lived through much of a period of discovery, I offer my thoughts on why I believe this past has something to offer the future.

In the following lectures, I shall talk primarily about the civilisations that shaped the history of the Southeast Asia region in which Singapore is located, and of which it is the centre. My focus will be on the many cultures that were developed within the region, and how the region had always been open to neighbouring civilisations.

This will include talking about cultures that have kept themselves separate — and have learnt to select ideas and institutions they needed for their cultures to shape their own distinctive identity. Singapore is no exception. It started later than the others, and given that its commitment to staying up front with modernity is very strong, its national identity is less clearly defined.

It is interesting how all the new nations use their historical experiences to help them build new national cultures, and how they expect to co-exist with modern and modernising civilisations. In this context, the region's nation-states have been engrossed with cultural adaptations, together with problems of nation-building, regional harmony and superpower rivalry.

To understand how they dealt with their problems and tried to keep up with a world of rapid changes, we need to examine the cultures developed here, and the kinds of civilisations they interacted with throughout the region's history. To try and do this, I believe that it is necessary to clearly distinguish the two words, "culture" and "civilisation".

But let me be clear. These lectures are not about the history of Singapore or Southeast Asia. They are about how the cultures of our region had lived with civilisations that shaped and enriched their local identities. They also look at how different civilisations interacted here in borderless ways. I use a historical frame to emphasise the processes of change and compare the different results the interactions have produced at different stages.

Civilisation for All

What do I mean by civilisation? How should it be distinguished from culture? Both are modern terms that came from Western Europe. The concepts have been translated into various local languages and are now commonly used. But the two are not always distinguished and, when in translation, are often used interchangeably. I have found it difficult to find satisfactory definitions of both words, so I shall describe what they mean.

Culture is what every group of people has shared because they developed it together and is something they identify as their very own. The groups could be large or small. They range from a simple one like an isolated tribe to a sophisticated community that could establish strong states. The cultures could be agrarian or pastoral, settled or nomadic, literate or non-literate. They were likely to be ruled by chiefs, priests, princes, kings and even emperors or elected leaders. Because their people of all classes had lived together for long periods of time, their cultures, whether defined as ethnic or national, were likely to be resilient and distinct.

Civilisation, on the other hand, stemmed from efforts by visionaries, prophets and teachers to explain the universe and find the meaning of life on Earth. From a set of first principles, ideational and moral systems were constructed to uplift the lives of everyone beyond local cultures and identities.

When such visions inspired the leaders of strong states and empires, those leaders could rise above their local cultures and use the idea of a common humanity to define a borderless civilisation under their care. Each would then seek to bring local states and cultures under their wing and act as an agent bringing civilisation to others.

Modern political discourse tells us that many of the early polities in Europe developed new ideas about the nature of their states. These led them to identify sovereign states that could determine national borders for themselves. The most powerful among them grew into national empires which, backed by a strong Christianising mission, claimed to be civilising the unenlightened. Many local European cultures grew to become national cultures and they went on to represent an imperial civilisation that reached out across the globe. By the 19th century, that modern civilisation began to impact all the cultures in Asia that they encountered. These included cultures under the umbrella of the ancient Indic and Sinic civilisations that were now relatively weak if not in decline.

After advancing to dominate the world, the credibility of this mission was diminished in the 20th century by two world wars. These were civil wars between rival national regimes that shared the same civilisation but had determined to destroy one another. However, the commitment to being modern was not affected. What emerged was a new world order created by the victors of World War II. This was designed to bring an end to national empires and replace them with a system of equal nation-states.

The ideal was to establish a single set of universally accepted values. But there was no agreement about what was universal. This led to an ideological division that brought about the Cold War between the United States (US) and the Soviet Union. When that ended, the US as victor became the world's superpower ready to spread its modern civilisation to all of humankind. It could choose whether to help the remaining ancient civilisations to modernise and survive, or have them integrated into the only civilisation there was.

Modern civilisation dominated all parts of our region during the 19th century. Before that, three ancient civilisations were influential until the 16th century, when the fourth arrived and quickly connected all the world's oceans. In my lectures, I shall focus on Southeast Asia, its cultures and their relations with the four civilisations. I shall begin by examining how the cultures that thrived were related to the ancient civilisations that impacted our region. I shall give special attention to the Indic civilisation that penetrated the region for more than a millennium.

My second lecture will take us to the Mediterranean where ancient civilisations of the three continents of Asia, Europe and Africa had met. I shall trace the Greco-Roman civilisation's transition to the two parts of an imperial monotheism. This will take us to how the bifurcated civilisations of the Christians and the Muslims came to interact in our region.

My third lecture will focus on the revolutionary changes that made Singapore a key port in an expanding British Empire — by then the largest of the national empires that extended modern civilisation around the world. I will also deal with the ancient civilisations that were losing control over their terrains. With Chinese merchants and coolies becoming dominant in Singapore, I shall also refer to the Manchu-Chinese Empire that grew alongside European expansion. This was when Sinic civilisation seemed to have peaked and then struggled to remain relevant.

In my last lecture, I shall look at how our region lived with civilisations after the end of World War II. Modern civilisation was already dominant while three ancient civilisations were trying to modernise. Of the three, China was rejuvenated after two revolutions in pursuit of modernity. That success has now made it a threat to American interests. In our region, Singapore has had to live with several civilisations when the city-state became independent. It chose an exceptional path by declaring its commitment to a "plural society" nationhood. How it embraced modern civilisation in a world where ancient civilisations are modernising has been a challenging experience and one whose future development deserves special attention.

Awareness of Cultures

I have now lived in Singapore for 27 years, and I have learnt to care for some aspects of its exceptional governance style and social structure. Most of all, I have become fascinated by its people's links with many different worlds. But this does not qualify me to talk about the governance of Singapore. I am happy that the S R Nathan Fellowship committee has allowed me to go beyond that subject.

What has struck me is the way Singapore and the region have been living with different cultures and civilisations. Singapore's experience is not unlike that of its neighbours in the region, but the differences are significant. Many commentators have looked at that phenomenon and I have gained much from the work that I have read. It has been a long learning process.

Let me begin with my personal background. I was brought up as someone Chinese who, failing to find home in China, tried to become Malayan, even Malaysian. I then wandered off to be Australian in Canberra, a capital city with a shorter history than Singapore, where almost everyone

I met came from somewhere else and only a tiny minority were actually born there. My work then took me to Hong Kong before I came to work in Singapore again. Everywhere I have been has been multicultural to a greater or lesser degree. So it probably is inevitable that my outlook is filled with cultural concerns.

I found it remarkable that the peoples of the region had each developed their distinct cultures while interacting with four civilisations. That historical response has continued to the present even while a powerful modern civilisation has been overwhelming ancient civilisations elsewhere. The peoples recognise that building new national cultures is of their tradition. How they modernise their cultures is through development and change. While Singapore may seek its own path towards creating its national culture, I believe that it found the region's experiences relevant.

I first learnt about Singapore as a student at the new University of Malaya, now the National University of Singapore (NUS). I returned as a lecturer from 1957 to 1959 before transferring to its Kuala Lumpur branch. This was when we all thought that Singapore would become part of the Federation of Malaya. When Singapore separated from Malaysia, I had to observe the country's development from outside. Thirty-seven years later, I came back to NUS through one of its research institutes. I have thus had at least three layers of Singapore experience. The first was at a site for higher learning, the second during an experiment in social engineering seen from afar and the third within a state engaged with modern civilisation.

Two images from my first stay have remained clear in my mind. One image came from the way the island was connected to the tip of the Malay Peninsula. I had seen that relationship captured by a name on some old maps I found in the university library. The name was *Ujong Tanah*, the endmost land. That picture of a long stretch of land sticking out to sea into the heart of a huge archipelago had followed me for decades. It led me every now and then to wonder about peninsulas and their role in history.

The other image came from my roaming the streets of Singapore. I met many people who had come to the island after wandering around the region,

Figure 1. Map of the Malay Peninsula, with Singapore as *Ujong Tanah*

Source: Ambrose Rathborne, *Camping and Tramping in Malaya: Fifteen Years' Pioneering in the Native States of the Malay Peninsula* (London: Swan Sonnenschein, 1898), 355. Courtesy of the British Library. This map is marked with Public Domain Mark 1.0.

and was introduced to a Minangkabau practice that caught my imagination. It is called *merantau* — a kind of wandering. What struck me was that *merantau* does not refer to travelling to a known destination. The wanderers, after years of seeking experiences and opportunities, expect to return home. In fact, on the contrary, many made a commitment to another land where they started a new life. I found the word *merantau* rich in meaning and closely linked to the peopling of this port city.

The two resurfaced images have led me to look afresh at the many unexpected connections Singapore has had to several worlds. The connections have helped me understand the plural societies in the region. It made me look again at the many peoples who became accustomed to living with one another. The idea of *Ujong Tanah* made me think about the genesis of cultures and civilisations. And when I deal with the peoples confronting modern civilisations in a globalised world, I shall come back to the idea of *merantau*.

As a history student, I had always found the idea of ancient and modern civilisations intriguing. I recall trying to understand how modern civilisation came from Europe to Asia. It led me to think that modern progress was desirable and ancient civilisations were backward, if not dying. The latter was painful to see but it seemed unavoidable. The Europeans we met expected to be helpful to all those who wished to modernise and become more like them. As an admirer of modern civilisation, I considered the university one of its pillars. I felt very lucky to be in a place where I could make myself modern.

However, my professors also taught me that if becoming modern enabled an Asian state to challenge the West, as the Japanese did in 1941, the Great Powers (Great Britain, the US and the Soviet Union) would be ready to hit it hard and put that power down. The lesson was that it was all right to learn from them and even try to copy them outright. But to think that the student could take on the master and drive him out of the region was unacceptable. Having studied Japan's ambition to dominate China and Southeast Asia, I thought that the defeat of Japan by the Western powers was deserved.

But back to the name *Ujong Tanah*. The idea of an island at the foot of the peninsula with people moving back and forth to the island linked me to my background in Malaya. I grew up on the peninsula side. My neighbours, including friends who went to the same school, were a mix of peoples who came originally from several worlds. Our teachers too had come largely from China, India and the Malay Nusantara world.[2] My parents both came from China and planned to return home as soon as they could.

My worlds had thus come to me from different origins. Two were linked to my English school in the state of Perak. The school regularly reminded us that we lived in a Malay Muslim sultanate that traced its origins back to historic Malacca and that Perak once had some tributary relations with the kingdom of Siam. But for reasons unexplained to us, my school was named after one of the governors of the Straits Settlements, a colony ruled by British Christian officials. At the time, I was not aware that no other school in Malaya was named this way. I realised later that it was an indirect and not too subtle way of telling us who was modern.

Both these worlds had little to do with the Chinese majority living in Ipoh Town. That community consisted of Nanyang *huaqiao* from the southern provinces of China. I recall how their different dialects, mainly Cantonese, Hakka and Hokkien, had made me wonder if there was more than one China. On the edge of town were Malay *kampung*, or villages, where people saw themselves as the Sultan's subjects, while the Indians I met were openly resentful of the fact that their homeland in India was under British rule. Only later did I understand that I was living with people who had different cultures. Some of the cultures were parts of ancient civilisations like the Indic of India, the Sinic that was developed in China, and the Islamic and Christian that had originated from the Mediterranean region.

To my bafflement, the relationships built on these worlds suddenly changed. From 1941 to 1945, Japanese armies took over the town. The new rulers did not trust the Chinese. They claimed to side with the Malays and won over many Indians to join them to drive the British out of India. Under Japanese tutelage, we heard slogans like "Asia for the Asians" and had to bow to the Emperor Showa. We saw that a civilisation like Japan with ancient Sinic roots could be modernised to fight back against those who claimed

---

[2] Nusantara refers to maritime Southeast Asia.

to be superior. I recall the relief among most people in Ipoh when the Japanese were defeated. But there was great uncertainty as to what would happen when the British gave up their empire and returned to their own country.

When I came to Singapore in 1949, I discovered that most of the people here had lived in worlds not very different from mine. Hence the delight when I saw maps with *Ujong Tanah* at the bottom of the Malay Peninsula. I could identify with that. It reminded me of how Singapore was Malaya's "Land's End". I knew that was just whimsy but there was a serious question there. How did this island at the tip of the Malay Peninsula fit into the region now called Southeast Asia?

I had just been made aware that Southeast Asia was the name for a region that never had its own identity. Few people today realise that this new University of Malaya was where the first books on Southeast Asia were produced. We were probably the earliest students anywhere to be taught that the region was of strategic interest to the Western empires. Before the war ended, even before the world agreed that the age of empires had come to an end, British strategists had identified the region around Malaya as essential to their interests in Asia. Looking ahead, they had seen the rise of a nationalistic China as inevitable. And they knew they would have to deal with an independent India with deep anti-British memories.

Two of our professors were enterprising and produced the first textbooks that introduced this region to the world. They were the geographer E. H. G. Dobby who published *Southeast Asia* (1964), and the historian Brian Harrison who produced *South-East Asia: A Short History* (1963).

I recall two of the discussions that followed the publication of their books. The first centred on the large peninsula between India and China that was nameless but unflatteringly known as Indochina. The peninsula also had a long extension, a narrow neck that led to a smaller peninsula. And its tip reached the island of Singapore that was to become of the country called Malaya.

Figure 2.   Map of Southeast Asia in Relation to India and China

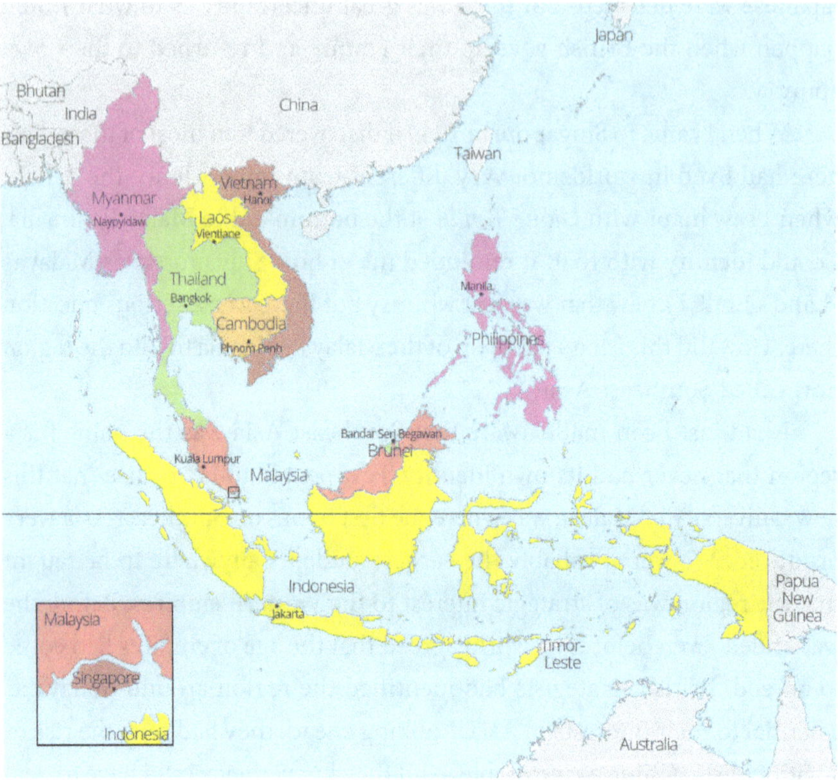

Source: ASEAN UP. Retrieved from https://aseanup.com/free-maps-asean-southeast-asia/.

The other discussion touched on the South China Sea. This was seen as a semi-enclosed sea that was connected from ancient times to the Mediterranean that was on the other side of the Indian Ocean. The people in the west had names for our region like Suvarnabhumi ("Land of Gold") and the Golden Khersonese ("Golden Peninsula"). Our region knew about the Mediterranean as the home of several ancient civilisations. This had led to suggestions that the South China Sea could be considered "Mediterranean". Was it not the meeting place of different ancient cultures and civilisations? Given that it had a huge peninsula stretching south to the Malay Peninsula in the middle of archipelagic Nusantara, why did the cultures there not gather their combined power and wealth together and create a civilisation?

Civilisations: Indic, Sinic and Islamic

The fact that they did not do so has to do with the question of how the region was peopled from ancient times. We now know that the first groups of people who came to dominate the region had come from China, south of the Yangtze River. The historical record does not identify them clearly but linguistic analyses show that these people spoke languages from at least three different language families, that is, branches of the Austro-Asiatic, the Austronesian and the Sino-Tibetan.[3] For that reason, southern China could be identified as "ancient Southeastern Asia", the home of tribes whom the Chinese records called the "Hundred Yue" and "Southwestern Yi".

Most of these tribes remained in China and are known today as minority "nationalities". Some had been Sinicised over time and become part of the Han majority. In ancient times, the earliest to move south into our region were the Austro-Asiatic who came overland and the Austronesian who travelled across the South China Sea. They were later followed by some Tibeto-Burman branches of the Sino-Tibetan, and others identified as Daic, who came to dominate the valleys of the Mekong, Menam Chao Phraya, Salween and Irrawaddy Rivers, each of them developing an agrarian economy and a separate culture. This is the area we now refer to as "mainland" (of Southeast Asia) and no longer as "Indochina".

Of the Austro-Asiatic, the Viet of the Red River valley lived under Confucian-Legalist institutions after their lands were conquered by Qin and Han empires. They developed a Sinicised culture after having been ruled by Chinese states for over 1,000 years. In contrast, the Mon and the Khmer came down the other river systems and established close relations

---

[3] One could add some from the Daic or Tai-Kadai language family that was related in various ways to the other three. Four of the Daic remain important today till this day: Thai or Dai, Lao, Zhuang and Shan.

with Indic civilisation[4]. Their elites were deeply inspired by Hindu-Buddhist teachers and advisers from India.

From Chinese records, we learn that a kingdom called Funan emerged at the Mekong Delta; another called Zhenla developed further inland. Later, the Khmer rulers built their remarkable empire and dominated the lower reaches of the Mekong for six centuries. Like Funan and Zhenla, this empire achieved its cultural heights by embodying localised versions of Indic civilisation. The Mon active in the Menam and Salween valleys also looked to India for their spiritual and artistic needs. Together with the Khmers, they laid the foundations for a deep and enduring Buddhist culture that is often seen as the most successful branch of Indic civilisation.[5] It is also worth noting that the Viet culture was also linked to India through the Mahayana Buddhism they shared with the Chinese.

The historical, artistic and architectural records show that throughout the mainland states, new ideas and institutions had come from various parts of the Indian subcontinent. What was striking was that the peoples of our region had their local genius. This enabled them to choose what they wanted to enrich and empower their own cultures.

There is no doubt that Indic prophets and teachers were the most dynamic and influential visionaries for centuries. You can see this in the two parts to the civilisation. There was the Dravidian core.[6] This was the indigenous civilisation in the southern parts of the subcontinent and it always had maritime interests in our region. And then there was the Indo-Aryan north that shared the continental visions of the Indo-European speakers of Central Asia.[7] Through the Hellenic and the Persian peoples who reached into northern India, those ancient links produced a world of multiple gods that was comparable to that of the later Greek and Roman civilisations.

---

[4] Mon refers to people mostly native to southern Burma.

[5] Some scholars did try to identify an ancient Khmer or Angkorian civilisation that was lost and rediscovered. However, following decades of research, it is clear that all the cultures developed on the mainland were inspired by ancient Indic civilisation.

[6] The Dravidian relates to a family of languages spoken in India, Sri Lanka and Pakistan, and the people who speak them.

[7] The Indo-Aryan are peoples who historically migrated from Central Asia to South Asia.

Figure 3. Khmer Devata Goddess Statue in the Preah Khan Temple in Angkor

Source: "Angkor, Preah Khan, Devata" by Arian Zwegers. This image is licensed under CC BY 2.0.

But unlike the peoples of the Mediterranean, those of the Indic civilisation did not find the monotheism of the Semitic peoples appealing. Indic civilisation was represented by people later described as Hindus who offered a distinct road to rebirth rather than visions of Paradise and Heaven. They focused on developing original and esoteric insights about life that most people in our region found attractive and inspiring. But their emphasis on rigid caste divisions did not take root. That is a clear example of how the countries in our region were selective in what they adopted into their local cultures.

Within India, there were many local states and cultures that were free to choose among the many paths available. Their deep-thinking teachers and priests debated fiercely among themselves. Their numerous states fought one another frequently. However, the civilisation continued to offer inspiration to those in our region who accepted what it had to offer. Its deep and rich cultural roots spread across the subcontinent, and its spirit of ideational and aesthetic inclusiveness enabled the civilisation to withstand external threats, first from the Islamic conquerors and later from the British Empire.

It is not clear what it was in Mon-Khmer cultures that found Indic civilisation so attractive. What we know is that when the Chinese first visited the earliest states on the mainland some 2,000 years ago, they recorded the strong presence of Indic institutions and a flourishing trade with the subcontinent. What was noteworthy was that the early Mon-Khmer rulers worshipped the gods of the Hindu pantheon, adopted Indic governance principles and embraced a wide range of Indic aesthetic values. But their descendants and the Siamese and Burmese successor states kept only the Buddhist realms of Indic civilisation.

The scholars who first studied the "Hindunised" states as they called them were fascinated to discover that the Nusantara peoples of the archipelago were no less influenced by Indic civilisation about the same time. Before, the mix of deities, governance methods, artistic artefacts and architectural monuments here were influenced in different ways by indigenous cultures. What was particularly striking was that when Indic contacts weakened, Buddhism did not survive there. Among the Nusantara peoples, the Hindu faith was left mainly in eastern Java and Bali. And contrary to what happened in India and among our mainland states, the archipelagic ruling elites eventually gave up much of their Indic heritage and turned to monotheistic Islamic civilisation instead.

This brings us back to the peoples who spoke varieties of Austronesian languages. These were maritime peoples that originated from different parts of the China mainland. It is widely agreed that they moved out of southern China by sea. Most of them originated from mainland China and island-hopped from Taiwan to the Philippines and beyond. Among them, some

Figure 4. Wayang Kulit Performance in Java

Note: This art usually depicts the tales of *Ramayana* in the Indonesian context.
Source: "Monolog story teller alias Dalang wayang kulit, the Javanese puppets show" by micro.cosmic. This image is licensed under CC BY-SA 2.0.

turned west to the coasts of central Vietnam where they followed the Khmers in accepting cultural influences from Indic civilisation and established their own riverine states. These became known as the kingdom of Linyi and then Champa.

Both the Khmer and Cham realms played a mediating role between archipelagic cultures and those of the mainland of Southeast Asia. Some of them crossed the South China Sea and stopped at the neck of the Malay Peninsula south of the Khmer Empire. There they created a frontier zone — a zone of contact — between the continental and the maritime that is still significant for the region today.

The people of Nusantara used their island world in different ways and kept their maritime trading activities distinct from that of earthbound mainland states. But both sides continued to develop their cultures by sharing the best of the Hindu and Buddhist manifestations of Indic civilisation. Neither the Khmers and their successors nor the archipelagic elites produced bold visionaries with independent worldviews that could have led to civilisations of their own. Both sets of states were content to shape their own respective cultures by selecting what they wanted from Indic civilisation. During the formative centuries of their development, they seemed confident that what they picked from that civilisation was sufficient to make them civilised and strong.

What is also worthy of note is that we learnt of their centuries of immersion in Indic political, religious and aesthetic values through Chinese records. About the same time, the Chinese had discovered that the Buddhist realm of knowledge and insights within Indic civilisation was wonderfully attractive and convincing. The expansion of their Nanhai trade in the South China Sea was largely based on the natural products collected by the Hindu-Buddhist peoples for their commercial needs. Large groups of Buddhist scholars from Sinic centres in China, Korea and Vietnam studied Indic civilisation in the old capital of Sri Vijaya, then at Palembang. They also moved among the local monks of the Singhasari realms of Java and its Mataram successor states. Like their counterparts in Southeast Asia, the Chinese saw civilisations as borderless and enriched their own cultures by choosing what to accept from other civilisations.

This takes me to our region's relations with early Sinic civilisation. Unlike with the Indic and its outreach across the Bay of Bengal, the core of the Sinic civilisation was in North China far away from the maritime world of the Nusantara peoples. The Chinese themselves had first received their share of Indic ideas and institutions from missionaries who came overland from Central Asia and northern India. From them, the Chinese were won over by the subtleties of Buddhist dharma. Where relations with our region were concerned, it was not until large numbers of Chinese had migrated to the southern coastal provinces of China that maritime commercial activities quickly began to develop.

After that, the Chinese reached out for the sources of the Indic worldview both overland through Southeast Asia's mainland states as well as by sea through the ports of the archipelago. Both merchants and officials profited from the growing trade. However, for centuries, it was the spiritual light of "Western Heaven" in India that drew the Chinese to our region.

From Fa Xian's travel account of the early 5th century to Yi Jing's two volumes on monks travelling to India via Sri Vijaya in the 7th century, there was enough testimony of the Indic magnet that stimulated Chinese maritime trade across the South China Sea. In comparison, the Indic-inspired Nusantara states left no major writings to record their ties with India but

Figure 5. Borobudur

Source: "Borobudur" by Seth Mazow. This image is licensed under CC BY-SA 2.0.

Figure 6. Prambanan

Source: "Prambanan_Temple" by threadytraveller. This image is licensed under CC BY-SA 2.0.

only scattered inscriptions to show the extent of Indic influence on local literacy. In any case, monuments like Borobudur, Prambanan and many others speak louder than words. Walking around those great sites of devotional architecture, who can doubt the depth that Indic spiritual and political penetration has reached?

When Buddhism lost its importance in India, China needed another kind of transformation to stimulate its commercial relations with our region. This came with the decline of the Tang Empire and the second period of division in Chinese history. From the 10th to the 13th century, the imperial state sought new sources of revenue and encouraged the enterprising people in its southern provinces to be more active in maritime trade. This meant that the trade received official support. We have more evidence of Chinese private trade pushing south to Luzon Island and the Sulu Sea, expanding commercial relations with Champa and the Khmer Empire, and extending their interests further to the ports of Java and Sri Vijaya. We also have Islamic sources of this period that confirm a growing trade involving the Chinese and the merchants from the Red Sea and the Persian Gulf.

All of those who traded with the Chinese learnt to value their manufactures like silk and ceramics and some of their trading methods and technological skills. But Chinese merchants had little capacity to reflect the political and cultural values of Sinic civilisation. In any case, it was clear that those values had little appeal to the Nusantara peoples who had been accustomed to an increasingly open multicultural environment. By that time, they were operating within the loose mandala system of state relations that they took from Indic civilisation. With that serving as a model, they had room to cultivate their own distinct local cultures.

Local Cultures

For the first thousand years of recorded history, our region was most responsive to Indic civilisation and adopted many elements of it to shape a large number of distinct cultures. Through a process that some have called syncretism, each set of rulers and their elites seemed to have gained cultural and political confidence by their success in shaping their local identity.

On the mainland, the Khmer and Mon, the Thai and the Burmese consolidated their Indic heritage through their respective versions of Buddhist authority after that had been lost in India itself. When they later became nation-states, that internalised authority provided strong foundations for developing modern national culture. Similarly, the Vietnamese, probably the first proto-nation in our region, were developing a distinct national culture drawing primarily from Sinic civilisation.

As for the archipelago peoples, their openness to all three of their neighbouring civilisations had enabled the local cultures on different islands and on the Malay Peninsula to retain distinctive features. This remained so even after most of its communities were later converted to Islam. Only those farthest to the east in the Philippines were later drawn into the Christian Mediterranean orbit but they too were inclined to maintain their own cultural features within that faith.

What began to make a difference was the growing importance of maritime power from the 16th century onwards. This power was shared between Britain and France during the 18th and 19th centuries. By that time, Southeast Asia was experiencing the early capitalist qualities of a

Figure 7. Goh Geok Yian, Associate Professor of History at Nanyang Technological University (at far right), Supervising Volunteers Excavating at the Fort Canning Hill Archaeological Site in the Area Now Named the Artisans Garden in 2018

Source: John N. Miksic and Goh Geok Yian, Site Report on the Fort Canning Dig 2018 (September 2–November 4) and Two Subsequent Visits, Figure 4. Retrieved from https://epress.nus.edu.sg/sitereports/fortcanning/text/excavation.

Figure 8. Statue of Admiral Zheng He

Source: Photo taken by Yudha P Sunandar.

modern civilisation that produced a decisive turn towards the idea of universal enlightenment.

Where was Singapore in all this? I imagine that there were always people on this peninsular island sweeping in and out and sharing the Indic civilisational experiences of the other Nusantara peoples around. Singapore historians with the help of archaeologists have taken its history back to the end of the 13th century, and you have seen artefacts that show the coming together of three civilisations. That was no accident. The century that is encapsulated in Fort Canning Park today saw important changes to the civilisational mix in the region.

The nomadic empires of Central Asia, Persia and Afghanistan had invaded the heartlands of Sinic and Indic civilisations with somewhat different results. On the one hand, Turko-Mongol forces diminished Indic influence at sea and supported Islamic presence in the Indian Ocean. On the other, total Mongol conquest of China encouraged southern Chinese to advance their trading activities beyond the South China Sea to India and the Persian Gulf.

The Temasek story linked the remnants of the Malay Sri Vijaya Empire to an emerging Javanese Majapahit Empire and the rising kingdom of Siam, all three born out of localised Hindu-Buddhist polities. Nothing before had prepared them for the naval expeditions under the Muslim Admiral Zheng He of Ming China that pushed beyond Singapore to support the establishment of Malacca. It has been suggested that the Muslims who headed the expeditions might have encouraged the Malaccan ruler to convert to Islam; but that probably mattered less than the fact that, at the moment in history, Islamic and Sinic interests converged. That laid the foundations for the Malacca Empire to become the base for Islamic maritime expansion.

We know little about the role of Singapore during the centuries of transformation that followed the arrival of Europeans. From time to time, the Nusantara peoples of the Straits and the archipelago tried to defend their interests from European expansion. For that, they would have used the island's harbour and rivers. Precisely what its place was among the contending elites from Malacca-Johor, the Minangkabau from Sumatra and the Bugis maritime traders of Sulawesi is unclear. That probably mattered less than the fact that the island was strategically situated when Anglo-Dutch rivalry led the two powers to separate their imperial interests once and for all in 1824.

By its very location, it can be said that Singapore was complicit in effecting that change. Something important was about to take place. The port city was on the frontline of national empires. The officials sent to run it believed that they were the standard-bearers of modern civilisation. What they were set to do would have massive consequences on the ancient civilisations that had so far been sustaining the region. In my next lecture, I shall explore the conditions that began to pave the way for revolutionary change.

Question-and-Answer Session
Moderated by Professor Kwok Kian Woon

Prof Kwok Kian Woon: Thank you Prof Wang for starting your series of lectures by placing your own biography within the longer-term historical context and, indeed, the wider geographical canvas. Thank you for also sharing your own personal links with *Ujong Tanah*, the endpoint tip of the peninsula and your own *merantau*, or wandering, which has also led to the questions you have put before us today. You have also laid out the foundations and the scaffolding for addressing these questions over the next three lectures.

Perhaps I will just make a quick observation. The concept of "civilisation" has often been met with suspicion by certain scholars because of connotations or claims about the superiority of any particular civilisation over others, including portraying others as being of a lesser state, sometimes as barbarians, or even as savages. But by framing the concept of civilisation with reference to deeper spiritual, intellectual and philosophical resources that we can draw from, and that continue to resonate with our own *merantau* as we face the contemporary world, I think that shifts the discussion in a very positive direction. That would be my one comment, but could I open the discussion please?

Participant: You mentioned both in your lecture and in the slides that the different parts of Southeast Asia — the different islands — were able to retain their distinct cultures. And for me the most interesting island in Southeast Asia is Java, and the question on my mind is why is it that the Javanese were able to create their own unique culture, which in a sense became the most successful culture within Nusantara and within the Indonesian fabric? What is it that made them different and allowed them to dominate Indonesia in the way that they do today? What was special about them that made them different from the people in Sumatra, in Borneo and elsewhere?

Prof Wang Gungwu: That is a question I've been asked again and again. It has been one of the most puzzling questions about our region. I have no simple answer to this. I believe that the most important reason is that those people who settled in Java very early had developed agriculture unlike elsewhere.

In all the islands, we read about riverine states. People never really went to the interior. Most of the people settled on the river close to the sea and concentrated their livelihoods on using the sea, either as fishermen, traders, smugglers or pirates. People of the Malay Archipelago essentially lived by the sea with the exception of Java. There was lots of land in Sumatra and Borneo, but the riverine people did not go inland and the people inland in these areas did not go into agriculture.

For example, the Dayak, Iban and Dusun in Borneo and the people in Sumatra who lived inland did not go into agriculture as much as the Javanese did. I recall one particular story. As you know I was born in Surabaya in East Java, and one of the stories I was told was that Java was different because if you poke a stick in the ground, it will grow because of the fertility of the land. The soil was volcanic, and Java was a set of volcanic mountains, which blew up regularly over millennia and left behind such fertile soil that all you needed to do was just put something in the ground and it would grow.

In the Malay Peninsula, in Sumatra and Borneo where it is mostly red laterite soil that we find, agriculture was not exactly appealing. It was hard work. Whereas life in Java as a peasant was relatively easy. This is my story, which I don't offer as a historical explanation, but I suggest that the agricultural success in Java made it more responsive to the kind of agrarian society that created the Indic civilisation in the first place. Indic civilisation was particularly successful among agrarian people. Even in China, it was agrarian people who responded to Buddhism. In mainland Southeast Asia, all the big riverine states, such as the Irrawaddy, Salween, Menam and Mekong, were very fertile and developed agriculture very early on. Indic civilisation thrived in all of them.

So, there may be a connection between agrarian societies responding to the agrarian origins of Indic civilisation much better. This includes the governance principles and the ideas of those gods, for example. They probably had to reflect a tremendous anxiety or desire to grow things fast and the deities helped to keep the land fertile and rich. Whereas maritime people like the Bugis or the Malay people generally turned to the sea.

Sri Vijaya is a very good example. We don't even have proper monuments of Sri Vijaya — the people just moved around from port to port. In fact, Sri Vijaya had different capitals around the Straits of Malacca and in the Riau-Lingga Archipelago — they never really turned to the land. They constantly changed their positions from one port to another and did extremely well. Even in the end when the Johor Empire began to revive itself, it was by the Bugis who came from thousands of miles away from Sulawesi. Again, they were people who used the sea but never really were attracted to life as peasants on the land.

As such, I would simply say as a possible hypothesis for further research that the agrarian fertility of Java made it easy for the people who settled there to become peasants. This then led to them having a different way of absorbing all the richness of the Indic civilisation so readily into Java.

Prof Kwok: Thank you, Prof Wang. This is a hypothesis that is worthy of a few more PhD theses.

Participant: Thank you for such a wide scaffolding anchored in the last thousand years of history. I'm encouraged by the comment made by Prof Kwok about civilisations, so I decided to ask about two themes which I hear emerging from your lecture. The first one is about Enlightenment and modernity, and the second is about the word you used, "pluralism", but that was more in the context of Singapore.

Clearly the Enlightenment in the 17th and 18th century, anchored in the Industrial Revolution and the rise of science, was compelling, but it doesn't necessarily extend to the world of humanities, ethics, politics and how to live. In the last 200 years or so, there is a sense that the Enlightenment as anchored in science was superior because it solved problems, but there are many issues (pertaining to ethics and humanity) which are now more evident. The rise of science without the rise of ethics and humanity and how to live is problematic in today's terms.

This brings me to the second question, which is about pluralism not just in Singapore, but the pluralism of civilisations. I'm curious on your views about how you view these questions on how to live with each other as civilisations, and want to ask for your comments on the rise of science as incomplete in itself. Do we need a more holistic view of what a civilisation means when it is framed as the Enlightenment?

Prof Kwok: Please remember that we have three more lectures! Prof Wang, the Enlightenment, the rise of science, and is there really a lack of or less development in the Western Enlightenment in the area of the humanities and ethics? And if so, is there something that we need to address here?

Prof Wang: There is no doubt that we need a holistic view of civilisation. I shall be talking about this in my next lecture, so I will say more then. But let me briefly say this about the Enlightenment. The major change occurred after the fall of Constantinople. Attitudes towards humanism and rationality did fundamentally change to bring about a Renaissance Europe, and that had its impact on the power of the Church and the states in Europe, power shifts that led to the Reformation.

The Enlightenment was the product of a series of conflicts within Europe, which were extremely cruel and brutal. In the course of sorting out their struggles, one thing became clear — there was a rejection of the absolute authority of the Church. That was the major turning point in the Reformation period between the Catholic Church and the Protestant world.

It included the end of the crusading wars of the Mediterranean against the Muslims when the Europeans ventured out of the Mediterranean into the Atlantic and Indian Oceans.

My next lecture will be about the global maritime, and it was the global maritime that created a different world. One of the first things to say about that was of course the opening of the Americas. That created a whole range of possibilities, such as new wealth, fantastic worlds and riches from gold and silver. The trade in Asia also blossomed, ultimately the secret of European success. Out of it all, the new way of living, which the Europeans encountered in the Americas as well as in Asia and elsewhere, stimulated tremendous excitement in Europe. Pulled together, they led to the war against the authority of the Church and further against that of the monarchs. In that context, the two followed logically. Once you have opposed the authority of some Pope or a Catholic Church that was absolute, you are open to reject other claims to authority, including claims to know the truth and the search for the truth, and this eventually led to the emergence of scientific thought. It's a long story and I'll come to that later. But you can see that it was a complete break and that was the beginning of what we call modern civilisation. However, it was a very special set of circumstances that created that and it had something to do with the breaking out of the Mediterranean into the Indian and Atlantic Ocean.

Participant: I was thinking about the definition of culture and civilisations that you drew. I wonder how you see the digital space that is growing and increasing in influence nowadays. Do you see this space as more of a culture or more of a civilisation? How would you place digital space in your definition?

Prof Wang: I don't think I have an answer. Modern civilisation produced one great difference from past expectations of the future. Modern civilisation believes in the idea of progress. That idea itself is actually quite extraordinary. No other civilisation had discovered that idea. In fact, all other civilisations referred to a golden age in the past from which they had deteriorated. They looked to the golden age to give them guidance and show them how to behave, because the past was always better than them.

The revolution came from this idea of progress — you believe that the future is going to be better than the past. Even in the great religions, when we talk about the future, there was always a day of salvation, and that future refers to somewhere else not on this Earth. So, the idea that material progress on this Earth is unending and will go on and on is probably the answer to your question on the placing of digital space. Where it's going to lead us to I have no idea.

Participant: My question is on language. You laid out very beautifully how different civilisations have impacted Southeast Asia at the cultural level. Can I understand your perspective on how language has influenced Southeast Asia through those ideas?

Prof Wang: As a historian, history only began when there was language — when there was literacy, which was used to create records. Only after we had records did we have history, so anything that was not written, we can only speculate on and we depend on archaeologists to do the work for us. But the question of language is indeed very important. Language essentially is rooted in cultures. Culture and language are inseparable and as I described in my definition of cultures, everybody has culture. Even the most primitive tribes have culture. They may not have civilisation, but they have culture. Culture refers to anything distinctive, which you share together as a group. And what you share together to start with is a spoken language, and what you share in common in the language provides you with the basis for culture.

When you have literacy, you advance that to another stage when you can actually have memory recorded for future reference, and this helps you become better by learning about the past — so you don't make the same mistakes you've written down. This allows you to pass knowledge down so that you can transmit it generation after generation. In this sense, literacy advances the borders of language, and people can communicate with a larger group. You don't have to know each other; you don't have to speak the same dialect. You can write it down and read it, so literacy adds this other dimension.

All this is still essentially a part of cultures. Every culture depends on some means of communication and language is the basis of it. Literacy to me is of course fundamental. Without literacy, there's no question of even acquiring civilisation. It is very difficult. How do you communicate something like civilisations? As far as I know, all the successful civilisations that have communicated have at some point or another been dependent on literacy.

Even for Indic civilisation in Southeast Asia, we don't have many proper records of what happened when Indic civilisation came here. We have it in monuments, aesthetics, the arts, music and dance, which have survived. The literacy part comes in inscriptions here and there. The people here in Southeast Asia did not have the tradition of keeping records but literacy gave them the ability to record history. We know the names of the rulers of Angkor, Mataram and Sri Vijaya because somewhere along the line there was some inscription which named the rulers in a script from India. No script as far as we can understand was invented in Southeast Asia. The speech may not have survived but the scripts have survived. And because the scripts survived, we can better understand civilisations by reading these scripts.

For example, we know how old the Malay language is not by what we read today in Rumi or in Jawi, but actually in Sanskrit. Sanskrit in Indic scripts has survived in some of the inscriptions in Sumatra. So, literacy then is essential to at least the transmission of civilisations. Cultures don't need literacy for that.

As I mentioned earlier, non-literate cultures can be just as rich in artistic and aesthetic forms, such as through things you create with your hands and what you do with your senses in terms of music and dance. There are many other ways of communicating culture, but civilisation, I think, ultimately depends on your ability to transmit a sense of the true meaning of life, how to become better people, how to improve ourselves and so on. These at least require some degree of literacy and in the end, the actual transmission does depend on literacy. All the civilisations that have survived to this day are highly literate civilisations. I'll come to this difference between culture and civilisation, and why it is so important even for Singapore. Singapore wants to develop a national culture, but the national culture could be based on many layers of civilisation.

Participant: You mentioned in one of your slides that in the early beginnings, Southeast Asia was a region with no identity. After more than five decades, what do you see as the identity of Southeast Asia? With the inclusion of Timor Leste, will this identity change and how will it affect the identity of Southeast Asia?

Prof Wang: As I said, the name was only invented in the early 1940s in the office of some British strategic thinkers during World War II. So, it is very recent. This region didn't even have a name and this is what I find so absolutely fascinating about it. It didn't have a name and yet when you look at the countries in the region, they had so much in common, including a deep base which was Indic in origin. There is a tremendous variety of this Indic origin in the region including Buddhism of course, and then layer after layer of Islamic and Sinic civilisation and ultimately of this modern civilisation which started as a European Christian civilisation, but which eventually developed into modern civilisation.

This region was always doing things differently from other places. Southeast Asia is located as a peninsula and an archipelago that did not have a unifying regional name. Even though the countries had common experiences, nobody bothered to give them a name until relatively recently. These are names which were invented to identify the countries in the region and the scholarly research of the last half century has been extraordinary in trying to reconstruct the history of Southeast Asia which didn't have a recorded history before. And now we see Southeast Asia as a region, which itself is of great interest and I shall come back to that.

Prof Kwok: Perhaps just to acknowledge that we have questions online — one of our listeners is asking about your key concerns surrounding modern-day civilisations, especially in the 21st century, with the rise of what has been called "radical worldviews".

Prof Wang: This is actually part of the idea of progress that I mentioned earlier on. Once you have the idea of progress and progress becomes a marker for what is modern, the modern has to be progressive. This involves improving ourselves all the time, advancing knowledge, getting a better sense of what is true and what is not true, and becoming more and more accurate about handling the most miniscule of things to the largest. To be able to do all that is a fantastic challenge.

Together with this idea of progress, what is beyond my capacity to understand is the way progress is gathering speed. In my lifetime, what I knew when I was young and what I learnt later on took me decades to fathom and to work out. With the technology that was available when I was young, I was in fact almost boastful of the fact that I didn't know how to use a telephone until I was 19 years old. But now if we look at how the world communicates, how do we compare that? And how do you measure the current speed of change compared to the speed of change in the thousand years before that, and in the thousands of years before that? That rate of speed of changes has shrunk to the point of being able to discover something new every day. Each day, something new is happening around the world and that can be communicated to you. This was unimaginable in my youth, and yet this is going to go on. Will it ever come to a stop? How do you reach the endpoint with this kind of progress of science and technology that we have now — I just can't imagine.

I have no idea what it's going to be like in the future, but I do know that the idea that we can progress by being creative and innovative constantly, as well as seeking to extend the frontiers of knowledge at the speed that we're going, make it seem like anything is possible.

Prof Kwok: Thank you, Prof Wang, and that's probably a partial answer to the earlier question about digital transformation.

Participant: You previously made some comments about empires. Today of course you've drawn our minds towards civilisation and culture. Earlier, the idea of Java was brought up and we know that Raffles and Farquhar were interested in Bangka, Karimun and Singapore as potential places to have a settlement. With all the wealth from Java, the Moluccas and the possibilities of Bangka, what was it about the Dutch civilisation and culture following the 1824 Anglo-Dutch Treaty that did not allow them to succeed in the way some of their competition did?

Prof Wang: There are other important words that I have not yet gone into, and the word "empire" is one of them. But even more important, and I shall come to that very carefully, is the word "nation". I have been talking about cultures and civilisation because they are always there. But empires came later and changed the definition of the word itself. I also argue that there are many kinds of nations. I will take up the point on empires and only deal briefly with it now.

Whenever one state becomes big enough and takes other people's states, it becomes an empire straight away. It can be a very small empire, and it can also be a very large empire. They range all the way from an empire which is no more than one state conquering the next state, to the empires that are global. For example, the British Empire was the first global one that incorporated seas, whereas the Mongol Empire was one that incorporated all the land that was available to them in Eurasia.

The changing way one controls power is grown in a way like knowledge and progress — by having the capacity to take in more territory, one's power and control become greater. However, what did change is that all those empires in one way or the other were dynastic empires. They had to do with one king, and succession depended on monarchies or emperors and their children in the family. Dynasties changed from time to time; one dynasty falls and another takes over.

In the next stage, there was the beginning of modern civilisation. This was when national empires developed. It takes us back to the word "nation" which was redefined as a nation-state. A nation-state consisted of the citizenry of a state where all citizens were masters in that state. There was no all-powerful king.

An empire like France or the US in the 18th century when it became independent was a completely new phenomenon. Today, this has become universal. Everybody now belongs to nations because those who were subjects of national empires wanted to be free from empires, and becoming independent nations was the way to do it.

"Anti-colonial" meant you had your own nation which was not part of a national empire. Those who wanted to be a nation in their own right took the word "nation". However, the problems of making ourselves nations were immense and varied from one country to another. They were much more complex than anyone realised. Those who started as anti-colonialists thought that they were going to be great at building nations. They thought that it was a job they had to do, that it was something they could all do, especially since their colonisers could do it. But nation-building was new to the whole of Asia and certainly to our region. It turned out to be an extremely difficult job.

As for the limitations of the Dutch, briefly, that had largely to do with the fact that the Dutch had continental rivals that could constrain their activities at sea while the British were on islands that were easier to defend from their enemies. I shall be dealing with that question in my next two lectures.

Prof Kwok: Prof Wang, you might just have set yourself up for another lecture series on empires and nations. I think in fairness to those who have joined us online, there are two questions that I will collapse together.

They have got to do with Prof Wang's idea of Southeast Asia and of course Singapore at the heart of Southeast Asia being the confluence of civilisations.

Prof Wang, you also spoke about mandalas, and there's a question asking about the implications of this confluence, especially from the vantage point of your generation, with these intertwining civilisations and intersecting histories. You of course were part of a generation that sought to create a national culture when Malaya was on the cusp of independence. I note that in your lecture you also spoke about a loss of political innocence on your part and this also translated into your later work. Could you leave us with some thoughts so that we will attend the next three lectures?

Prof Wang: That's a big pile of questions out there. But let me try and use one particular point, which I think is very important and I believe is central to many of our problems today. This is my understanding of civilisations as being borderless.

If a civilisation is able to produce or provide high-quality ideas, brilliant discoveries and methodologies — the inspiration of some spiritual, intellectual or even physical change that everybody aspires to and is impressed by — all that is actually borderless. If anybody can learn it, it is like the diffusion of knowledge. Once a civilisation provides that knowledge, it's not that hard for people to pick it up because nobody stops them. What we're up against when you have things like empires and nations and particularly nations is to have borders that not everyone can cross. Nations are now part of a system that the world has found to be necessary. Once you have these nations, there are systems of laws, regulations, prohibitions, all of which add up to affect the idea of borderless civilisations. Human beings have profited from modern civilisation just as their ancestors had from borderless ancient civilisations.

Modern civilisation was borderless, and it was spread by national empires when they conquered the world. On the whole, it was borderless in the sense that we could all learn from them. The Europeans who came out to Asia were very happy to teach us. They were quite happy to do that because they were confident and they were not afraid. In fact, they were very happy that people wanted to learn from them. They only became fearful when they realised that others could learn from them and become even better. This fear gave way to borders, where one begins to dictate what others can and cannot learn. Once this happens, there is a movement away from civilisation. That is no longer civilisation but more like imperial or nationalistic talk. Once there is a fear of being borderless, we are no longer talking about civilisation, but about national cultures fighting against each other. I'll come back to this word "borderless". I will be talking about that because it covers many of the problems that we face today.

Prof Kwok: Thank you, Prof Wang. I'm so glad I allowed a little more time. This seems to me a very good place to end, with the concept of civilisation and the idea of borderlessness, and transcending borders being in some ways both intellectually and socially liberating. I think one takeaway for me is that we live on an island but we don't have to think like an island — we can think in relation to the peninsula, to the archipelago and to the wider world.

Prof Wang, you said at the end of the lecture that your next lecture will explore the conditions that paved the way for revolutionary change. You left us with a cliffhanger and we are all awaiting your next lecture with great anticipation. Thank you, Prof Wang, for this excellent session.

Lecture II
OPENING TO THE GLOBAL MARITIME

LECTURE II

In my last lecture, I focused on the rise of local archipelagic and mainland cultures to show why the peoples of our region shared a remarkable confidence in their ability to define their local identities. This confidence enabled them to interact readily with their neighbouring civilisations. Of the three that influenced the region's early development (i.e., Sinic, Indic and Islamic), the Hindu-Buddhist under Indic civilisation had the deepest roots going back more than a thousand years. The imperial Chinese or Sinic from the north and east came later and its impact was limited to material culture. The Islamic Mediterranean from the west across the Indian Ocean was most successful among the maritime peoples.

From the start and for all parts of the region, Indic civilisation was favoured. It grew deep roots because it seemed to have had comprehensive appeal, especially among the agrarian peoples of mainland Southeast Asia. Even when the local peoples established links with the Sinic or Chinese civilisation to the north, what they found they had in common was their devotion to the Buddhist worldview that came from India. As for the Mediterranean world further west, our region's contact with it was initially confined to trade, and it was because of the openness of the maritime areas that merchants from the Red Sea and the Persian Gulf were attracted to our region in the first place. However, when Islamic power led by the Persians and Turko-Mongols came overland to dominate northern India, the influence of the Indic civilisation on our region began to diminish.

I suggested in my last lecture that the 13th century was pivotal. The bearers of both the Sinic and the Islamic civilisation became more active and their impact on the life and cultures of the archipelago became prominent. What was striking was the way the Southeast Asian mainland and the archipelago peoples responded differently to changes in civilisational contacts. They each chose what they thought would enhance their quality of life and make their respective local cultures stronger and more distinctive.

On the mainland itself, there were a variety of responses to the neighbouring civilisations that influenced our region. The Vietnamese elites retained the core ideas of the Sinic civilisation but kept a clear political distance between their dynastic state and Chinese imperial power. Yet, the small coastal Cham states to their south — the Cham being Austronesian-speaking people who inhabited Central and South Vietnam — continued to take their cultural values from Indic civilisation. However, they were careful to draw clear lines between them and their Khmer neighbours. At the same time, Cham rulers fought the Vietnamese to their north. After the 15th century, the Cham peoples began to lose their lands to a Vietnamese empire, but they retained their Indic maritime culture and did not change their way of life. Later on, when their Malay cousins of the archipelago turned to embrace Islam, they also chose to do the same.

Such developments were not observed with the Khmer and Mon peoples from Cambodia across to Southern Burma. For reasons that are still unclear, they discarded the Hindu core of their Indic civilisation. This was surprising when you see in the monuments of the Angkor Empire how much was done to portray its glorious Hindu features. But although direct Indic influence was lost, it is remarkable how strong it remained in the Buddhist cultures that flourished thereafter. When new groups of peoples migrated southwards from Yunnan in China and the Tibetan highlands with their own Indic Buddhist faiths, much of our region's mainland was transformed. In different ways and at different times, the various Siamese dynasties of Ayutthaya and the Pyu-Myanmar peoples of the Pagan and Ava empires established Buddhist states to succeed the weakened Khmer imperial realms, which were primarily Hindu.

And as you may know, I have been highly selective in my references to history. They are limited to what illustrates the shaping of local cultures that had drawn on ancient civilisations for inspiration. These lectures are not about our region's history but about a particular phenomenon that is still relevant and may become even more so as the modern world order faces new challenges. I now come to the period when stronger forces from afar begin to impact on the region.

There were major changes taking place in both China and India. I mentioned earlier that invaders from continental Asia led to Islamic control over large parts of northern India. As for China, there were the nomadic armies of north and central Asia, especially the Khitans, Jurchens and Mongols, who harassed the Chinese dynastic state. That was the time when the Song state was forced on the defensive as a relatively weak power. This led its Neo-Confucian philosophers to concentrate on revitalising the very foundations of Sinic civilisation in order to protect and promote its great heritage.[1] Although they established what became a new orthodoxy of Chinese values for the next 700 years to the 19th century, the rulers of the Song dynasty failed to save the remaining provinces of China from being conquered by the Mongol, Kublai Khan. In short, during the 13th century, new forces from the west via India and from the east via China provided severe tests for the local cultures of our region, both on the mainland and in the archipelago.

---

[1] The revived Confucianism of the Song period (often called Neo-Confucianism) emphasised self-cultivation as a path not only to self-fulfilment, but also to the formation of a virtuous and harmonious society and state.

The Open Sea: Age of Commerce

More changes were to follow and the rest of this lecture will deal with a new set of maritime peoples who circumnavigated the world by crossing massive oceans. The period covers the centuries leading to the 18th century when our region experienced what Anthony Reid calls the "Age of Commerce". From the perspective of civilisations and cultures, the period might also be described as the age of the fourth civilisation. It marked the growing presence of the Christian half of the monotheistic Mediterranean civilisation. That had been a constant rival to the Islamic half and was seen in our region as a separate civilisation.

Let me outline some notable events following the coming of this Christian civilisation brought first by the Portuguese and the Spanish. Our mainland polities of the Mon, Burmese, Shan and Tai noted their arrival and, for the next three centuries, kept these foreigners out and chose to concentrate on fighting among themselves to consolidate the distribution of power on the mainland.[2] The Buddhist kingdoms did welcome Portuguese help with superior weaponry but were not attracted to their Christian civilisation. They remained connected with Indic civilisation even though Buddhism was no longer of importance on the Indian subcontinent. Through sustained contacts with Sri Lanka, the traditions of Theravada Buddhism were regularly nourished.

Siamese rulers in particular were aware that the Europeans offered different ideas and institutions that might be useful for their political needs. For example, the Ayutthaya king Narai did establish an informal alliance with France against the expanding Dutch and English trading companies. But despite both sides making efforts to benefit from increased contacts, the Siamese elites remained unmoved by what the Jesuit scholars had to

---

[2] Tai is a large group, which includes Thai, Lao and Shan tribes. Shan refers to those now living largely in Myanmar.

offer. In comparison, the Burmese were interested in Portuguese military firepower and little else.

The Vietnamese were more open to new ideas coming from Europe, notably among those in the south, along their southern frontier areas furthest from the Chinese Sinic core. However, for the literate officials, the new civilisation was politely received but the influence was limited.

As for the rulers of maritime Southeast Asia known as Nusantara, most of them had converted to Islam before the Iberians of Portugal and Spain arrived during the 16th century. The Muslim states that were already established were drawn both to the faith as well as to trade and economic advantage. There was a replacement of the formal political institutions that had been inspired by Indic civilisation, but some of the new Islamic influences were also coming from India. This can be observed in the Sufi religious teachings from India which gained influence in North Sumatra, a part of the Nusantara. I still remember how impressed I was when, as editor of the Malaysian Branch of the Royal Asiatic Society, a profound work was brought to my attention. This was the study of the attempt by Nuruddin Al-Raniri from India of the 17th century to counter the insights of a local Indonesian Sufi poet Hamzah Fansuri. Although only incidentally, that work captured for me the quality of the philosophical concerns about Islamic civilisation that the ruling classes in the Malay world were already drawn to appreciate.

At the same time, I was also reminded, by visits to the historic sites of Java and Cambodia, how much of the Indic visual arts and the aesthetics deeply lodged in our region's cultures have survived. The peoples on the mainland and in the archipelago were clearly comfortable and confident about the integrity of their earlier local responses to different civilisations. Their domesticated cultures had helped them to manage their relationships with the Sinic and Islamic civilisations that came later. It seemed to me that their experiences also taught them to treat new civilisational manifestations as unthreatening to their fundamental beliefs.

It is with that background in mind that I have approached the question of how our region responded to the arrival of the Portuguese and the Spanish, and then the trading companies of the Dutch and British, and later that of the French. When Portuguese explorer Vasco da Gama and his fleet reportedly said they had come for "Christians and spices", they added an additional religious dimension to what had been a largely Indic trading environment, enlivened by a localised framework with a strong Islamic edge. This can be seen in the way the Undang-Undang Laut Melaka, or Maritime Laws of Melaka, were respected by merchants of Indic, Sinic and Islamic backgrounds alike.

It has often been taken for granted that the arrival of the Portuguese and the Spanish marked a turning point in the region's history. Some historians have gone further to suggest that it was an early marker of the

Figure 1.   Angkor Thom

Source: Retrieved from https://www.freepik.com/free-photo/historic-statues-angkor-thom-siem-reap-cambodia_11207073.htm.

rise of a global modern civilisation. But there was actually nothing modern about this Iberian mission. What it signalled was the arrival of the Mediterranean heritage of the "civil wars" between two alternative paths to a common monotheistic faith.

Coming with well-armed ships into the Indian Ocean, the Portuguese brought with them centuries of Catholic European hostility against their Islamic rivals. By that time, the Muslims in Asia, especially those of the Red Sea, the Persian Gulf and the western coasts of India, were looking to the Ottoman Turks in Istanbul for leadership and were determined to respond violently in return. As we know, their deadly struggles to represent their faith in the archipelago saw the Portuguese take over Muslim Malacca and then go on to control the Maluku Spice Islands.

Singapore was part of that struggle, especially when the Malaccan forces tried to defend their new base up the Johor River. After that failed and they moved south to the Riau-Lingga Archipelago — further away from Singapore — Singapore became merely one of the many ports that were affected by the wars that continued for the next two centuries. Merchants from the Indic and Sinic worlds continued to trade in Portuguese Malacca. The Orang Laut and others in Singapore would have been aware of the civilisational conflict taking place around them, but they lived mainly with Nusantara Islam. That would have given them some sense of security because the civilisation of the caliphate, which was the headship of the Islamic faith, had by that time developed a large footprint on our region.[3]

As Indic Buddhist local cultures remained strong on the mainland and Islamic economic influence was growing in the archipelago, we find Sinic civilisation undergoing unexpected changes that would affect Chinese relations with our region. In my last lecture, I mentioned the Mongol conquest and the consequent spread of Eurasian power that changed the nature of Sinic civilisation. In addition to changes to the map of China, the

---

[3] Caliph is typically used to refer to an Islamic ruler who looks over the political and religious affairs of an Islamic community. Territory ruled by a caliph is known as a caliphate.

long-distance outreach of Chinese coastal merchants, and to the further expansion of Islamic civilisation in our region, there were at least three other shifts of historical significance after the 14th century.

First, the Ming Chinese rulers were drawn back by the northern Mongol threats, and that led them back to a continental worldview. Second, the Koreans and Vietnamese saw how the Chinese had failed to defend Sinic civilisation against the Mongol "barbarians". For the Japanese, that total Mongol conquest only confirmed their belief that they had been right all along to choose only those bits of Sinic civilisation that enhanced their own cultures. Third, the coastal Chinese settlers in the south had to re-learn ways and means to advance their maritime ambitions and adopt new ways to deal with the European commercial empires that now appeared on their shores.

From across the South China Sea, the Ming rulers had supported the rise of Islamic Malacca and sent the Muslim Admiral Zheng He to lead seven expeditions to the Indian Ocean. But when they were satisfied that there were no enemies out there, the powerful fleet was withdrawn and destroyed. The Chinese authorities did continue to be watchful of external maritime contacts, but they prohibited their own merchants from trading overseas. This forced foreign trade to be conducted through a highly bureaucratised tributary system. This was so institutionalised that it is now often presented as a Chinese "world order" that the Chinese might want to restore.

However, its contemporary impact was not much more than to ensure maritime security by restricting private trade on the China coasts. Fortunately for the coastal provinces, the local mandarins knew that it was not in their interest to curtail merchant enterprise to that extent.[4] They were often lax with their controls and thereby made it possible for considerable Chinese private commerce to thrive.

---

[4] Mandarins can refer to public officials in imperial China.

The Buddhist states on the mainland had no difficulty with the system and the Siamese kingdom in particular continued its profitable relations with the Chinese. The tributary system certainly did not affect trading connections between mainland Southeast Asia and various Europeans nor did it prevent them from developing links with Muslim merchants. As mentioned earlier, the Siamese, Mon and Burmese rulers did establish trading relations with the Europeans to advance their ambitions down the Malay Peninsula. But they were unable to avoid their own deadly wars and thus never posed a serious threat to the areas further south. What was more serious for Nusantara Islam was the way the Catholic powers and their caliphate rivals extended their antagonistic relations into our region. Here our region encountered a bifurcation of civilisational linkages.

The Sinic formed a different set of relationships with the Europeans as compared to with our region. In a transactional approach peculiar to the governance of Ming China, the Portuguese were allowed to administer Macao as the only port city open to foreign private trade. This was an intriguing development. It gave the Portuguese an advantage that made them more than equal to their rivals who had to operate through the tribute system.

Further east, Hokkien Chinese had access to Luzon and this helped the Spanish obtain spices and even convert some of the Chinese to Christianity. And through the Manila Galleon trade with Mexico, the Chinese manufactures in great demand in Europe were also able to reach those markets beyond the Pacific Ocean. In short, despite the official restrictions by Ming authorities, Chinese merchants were increasing their commercial influence.

Trading activities for much of the region were forced to adapt to the regular battles involving the Christian–Muslim rivals, but they could still be conducted in the old familiar ways. The list of traded goods grew longer and, in time, the major players from the Mediterranean came to concentrate on gaining profits and cared less about saving souls. Local elites also became more skilled in dealing with the different factors that guided foreign ventures in their territories. However, the four civilisations now in contact with one another in the region, the Indic, the Sinic, the Islamic and the Christian European, were still interacting on the same trading platforms and, whether violently or peacefully, were still competing in similar ways.

Here I believe we can say that our region's confidence in their local cultures while interacting with expanding civilisational interests helped them to manage their relationships with considerable skill. The fact that their earlier partners or competitors of Sinic or Islamic origin were not considered threatening to their cultures was a vital factor in their resilience.

The Fourth Civilisation: Christian European Civilisation

This brings me to the Europeans who first arrived on the Malabar Coast, located on the southwestern coast of India. Theirs was a composite Mediterranean civilisation that had grown out of ancient civilisations in

Figure 2. Angengo Fort on the Malabar Coast

Source: "The north east view of Angengo Fort on the coast of Malabar" by Wellcome Collection. This image is licensed under CC BY 4.0.

Africa and Asia, along the two river systems of the Nile and the Tigris-Euphrates. In the study of history, we now have a fuller record of how the civilisations have crossed communal, cultural and political borders; how several cultures can produce a new civilisation and how two civilisations can interact and converge into one more inspirational civilisation.

I recall my time as a history student when I saw Southeast Asia's mainland as a large peninsula that did not produce its own civilisation. The mainland's narrow peninsula with Singapore-Malaya as *Ujong Tanah* did not unite it with the archipelagic world, but actually served as a dividing space between the maritime and the continental, one that was further underlined by civilisational (mainly Buddhist and Islamic) differences. I was led to contrast our region with the enclosed Mediterranean that had several prominent peninsulas, with each of them contributing to the struggle for civilisational supremacy.

The largest were those of Anatolia (located on the Asian part of today's Turkey), Italy, Iberia (the peninsula where Spain and Portugal are today) and Greece, where other small peninsulas and islands make an exceptionally spiky peninsula. Over time, the cultures that developed in each of them contributed political resources to a Mediterranean civilisation. The peoples had come from different directions: the Semitic peoples of the east and south who spoke Hebrew and Arabic; the Indo-Europeans of continental Eurasia and northern Europe and the indigenous peoples of North Africa. Over the centuries, they had evolved their varying belief systems, from having many gods to different perspectives of a monotheistic faith. Hence emerged over millennia the exclusivist Hebrew, the mission-driven Christians and the self-purifying Islamic *Ummah* ("community of believers"). Eventually, it was the similar monotheism that laid the foundations of a deeply interlocked and dynamic Mediterranean civilisation.

I was intrigued by how this happened. The peninsulas were constantly challenged within a claustrophobic sea. Under pressure from the empires of Assyria, Babylon and Persia, the Anatolian peninsula provided an opening to the coastal waters that enabled them to confront the Greek city-states. In response, the city-states and their maritime colonies organised themselves to resist the Persian Empire. Eventually, the Greeks produced their own intercontinental empire under Alexander the Great. This enabled the Mediterranean civilisation to turn eastwards and conquer continental territory in India and Central Asia.

The flowering of that imperial Hellenistic power stimulated the rise of an even more powerful Roman Empire on another peninsula — that of Italy.[5] Its expansion, which spread west to Iberia and the whole length of North Africa, led to Italy's control of the Mediterranean Sea for several centuries. However, after the 7th century, the successor states of this empire succumbed to an explosive Arab power in the eastern Mediterranean that created their distinctive Islamic cultures. For more than seven centuries after that, the Abbasid caliphate dominated its southern coasts and was later reinforced by freshly Islamised Turkic invaders from Central Asia who steadily expanded westwards.

In the face of these advances, the European Christian lords launched their Crusades and fought for centuries to drive out the Muslims and retake the holy city of Jerusalem. They also hoped to get direct access to the wealth of India. But their efforts were in vain. It was not until the 15th century when the Muslims captured Constantinople, and the Spanish drove the Muslims out of the Iberian Peninsula that the European half of the Mediterranean finally freed itself from that long confinement within the Mediterranean peninsulas. The kingdoms of Portugal and Spain sponsored the adventurers who took Mediterranean civilisation out across the open oceans, both finding their New World and both pushing further to connect with the Asian continent.

This Iberian moment in our region was tied to the quest for the Spice Islands and the wealth for those who could control their access. No less

---

[5] Hellenistic describes Greek history, culture or art during the period after Alexander the Great.

Figure 3. Map of Mediterranean Peninsulas (Mediterranean Basin) (1982)

Source: Courtesy of the University of Texas Libraries, The University of Texas at Austin. Retrieved from https://maps.lib.utexas.edu/maps/europe/mediterranean_rel82.jpg.

Figure 4. Map of the Crusades

Source: "Early crusades" by Norman B. Leventhal Map Center at the BPL. This image is licensed under CC BY 2.0.

important was the mission to find Christian allies against the Muslim powers. But apart from a small number of Christian communities on the Malabar Coast, there were none to be found. Instead, finding heathen Chinese and Japanese was a great challenge and that did lead the faith warriors from the Catholic powers to try to make new Christians. For reasons that had to do with the deep gulf between civilisations, most of their efforts kept raising conversion hopes but largely came to nothing during those early centuries.

The Spanish friars who went westwards were more successful. They said less about trade and spices but concentrated on extending their mission across the Pacific to the Philippines. They were fortunate to reach the islands before the Muslims had advanced very far and were able to convert most of the indigenous peoples. As in the Mediterranean, the Catholic powers rarely succeeded in converting those who were already Muslim. This reminds us of their origins as a composite civilisation separated by different measures of God's truth. The divisions were deepened when they met outside the Mediterranean while encountering other civilisations. I shall not deal here with what followed, that is, post-Renaissance Europe and its secular modern civilisation; that will be the subject of my last two lectures.

To sum up, the arrival of well-armed Portuguese ships led to conflict wherever they met their Muslim competitors. This led to a disruption in existing trading conditions. The Portuguese had to build fortified ports and depended on naval firepower to resolve any issues of contention. By so doing, they were never free from fighting old crusading battles and, to put it simply, they failed to sustain the commercial advantage that they had when they controlled the Spice Islands and held the monopoly position in Macao. It was left to their successors from northwest Europe to develop a mercantilist emphasis on trade that eventually produced the civilisational challenge to everything that the region had been accustomed to in the past.

Capitalism and the Idea of Progress

Something new — identified later as capitalism — was taking over from older trading conventions in Western Europe, and it ultimately led to important transformations around the world. This began with the globalisation of sea power. It had begun with the Iberians breaking out of the Mediterranean and crossing both the Atlantic and the Pacific, as I mentioned earlier. But they were primarily royal and imperial exercises that took pride in their conversion of indigenous peoples, and were largely satisfied by the acquisition of precious metals like gold and silver. It was not until a century later that a new breed of adventurers, mainly Protestant Christians, came to focus their attention primarily on the profits of trade.

In the Netherlands and England, these merchants chafed at the limits of royal and church patronage and developed the trading organisations that emerged in Asia as the English East India Company and the Dutch East India Company. The companies sought support from the state and its nobles to gain a monopoly of long-distance trade and created the best possible conditions for the merchant classes to work in. By combining naval power with innovative financial institutions, the two companies began to change the economic framework of their own countries as well as those in parts of our region.

On the surface, this might seem to be no more than a new way to make fortunes, but it was more than that. It introduced the practice of state-protected private enterprise and may be seen as the young shoots of a new kind of political economy. The calculations that propelled the Companies to pursue material wealth in this way could be described as the product of a modern mind, one that was not burdened by the traditions of church and state and concentrated on profitable outcomes. In the historical discourse of European civilisation, that development was the outcome of major reinterpretations of Christian gospel and a by-product of major conflicts among powerful religious and political interests.

Figure 5. Dutch East India Company Ship Painting

Source: "Ship of the Dutch East India Company" by Thomas Quine. This image is licensed under CC BY 2.0.

For the first stage of the move towards modernity, it had begun with the Roman Church defending against a triumphant Ottoman Empire that led to the rise of Renaissance Europe. Then came the Christian wars between Catholic powers and Protestant kingdoms. This was the product of the Reformation and was challenged by several religious orders of the Counter-Reformation. The long list of wars and the voluminous literature devoted to sorting out rights and wrongs was accompanied by many controversies over what triggered the new kind of Christian thinking. The next stage towards modernity — the critical thinking that gave birth to the Age of Enlightenment — was the work of powerful minds that brought fundamental changes to an increasingly dynamic world.

However, for the three centuries after Vasco da Gama's arrival in India, there were very few indications in Asia that the ruling elites were aware of the changes happening in Europe. There were European accounts of their priests conversing with powerful leaders of Mughal India, Ming Chinese and Qing Manchu emperors and making an impression on some of them. But it is doubtful if any of the rulers in our region thought it necessary to watch out for what was about to transform the West into a powerful force for the future.

Those directly involved in the European trade were ready to respond to the growing markets for new commodities like tea and cotton textiles in Europe as well as the opium addiction that created a massive market in China. We can assume that they were all happy with the news that trading volumes rose rapidly as more European merchants joined in the competition for profit during the 18th century. Nothing in our region's records suggest that there was any awareness that a modern civilisation was on the horizon.

If anything, the contrary was true. When the French version of the East India Company arrived in Asia during and after the reign of King Louis XIV, they acted more like the Iberians before them. They were accompanied by militant priests and reminded our region that there was a part of Europe that was still committed to bringing its Christian civilisation to Asia. It is also interesting that the French missions concentrated on the heathen of Indic and Sinic civilisations and usually left their Islamic rivals of the archipelago alone.

This brings me back to the strong cultures in our region that had over the centuries learnt how to handle the ancient civilisations that they had earlier encountered. The different areas of our region had each shaped their distinct cultures so well that the people remained confident that their heritage was sound and capable of dealing with what new groups of Europeans were bringing to the region.

First, there were the Southeast Asia mainland states that shifted their Indic heritage from Hindu gods and institutions to the worship of the Buddha. Although they reached the ocean and their ports traded across the Gulf of Siam and the Bay of Bengal, the internecine wars overland among themselves were far more important in determining the fate of their countries. The kingdom of Ayutthaya in Siam pushed farthest south to advance its maritime interests and was the most active in dealing with European maritime trading companies. But even they had to turn regularly

Figure 6. Map Showing Bay of Bengal, Gulf of Thailand (Siam) and Myanmar (Burma)

Source: "DSC0001/Burma/Shan Table Land/Shan Plateau Map" by dany13. This image is licensed under CC BY 2.0.

inwards to deal with incessant threats from their continental neighbours, especially from the Burmese.

In comparison, the peoples of the archipelago were far more responsive to newcomers to the region. Being oriented to the seas, they had always been more open and inclusive. With that background, they observed how the Dutch outdid their rivals of Banten in West Java, and even offered support to the Dutch to ensure the defeat of the Portuguese in Malacca. They also found it easier to trade with the East India Companies after the Portuguese were edged out of the Spice Islands.

The Dutch and English merchants did not portray themselves as enemies of what the Nusantara peoples accepted as Muslim civilisation. It was enough that their company agents were proud of their own European civilisation that was no less ancient and distinguished as the Islamic. But they had responded to the Reformation divide in the Christian churches and rejected the Iberian obsession with crusades and holy war. Instead, with the support of their political leaders, they concentrated on developing a commercial framework in Asia, within which religion and other civilisational factors were handled with a degree of sensitivity.

It is interesting to see how the local cultures interacted positively with these foreign protagonists. Our region's own trading classes also did their best to ensure that business relations would be profitable. A good example of this was the way Muslim Johor stood with the Christian Dutch against their Muslim rivals in the Acehnese Empire. Another was how the Dutch were quick to note that Chinese private traders who were equally uninterested in religious differences were already established in various parts of the archipelago. When they realised that these Chinese were ready to respond to the new opportunities that their East India Company could provide, valuable partnerships were set up to expand their respective outreach wherever they could. As the Dutch were keen to advance further east to the China coasts, Taiwan and Japan, such cooperation proved to be very advantageous.

The English Company in turn shared a similar outlook about civilisational differences. Their early conflicts were primarily with their Dutch rivals over access to the Spice Islands. When they saw better opportunities for their products on the Indian subcontinent, they shifted their focus. There they found that all sides, whether Indic, Islamic or Christian, appreciated it when attention was paid primarily to commercial dealings. Where China was concerned, despite the Portuguese monopoly in Macao, they developed a monopoly of the tea trade with the Hong merchants of Canton. Again, civilisational differences were carefully set aside to ensure maximum profitability on both sides.

In our region, Nusantara entrepreneurs continued to advance their interests in Sumatra and the former Malacca territories. The people who

Figure 7. Map of Nusantara with the Spice Islands at the Eastern End (1729)

Source: Herman Moll, *The Philippine islands and others of the East Indies according to newest descriptions,* National Library of Australia, Bib ID 601352.

lived and worked in Singapore probably shared the pragmatic outlook of those in the Johor Empire and responded to whatever changes were necessary to match the Dutch challenge. But, for most of the 17th and 18th centuries, the local cultural elites did not think that this fourth civilisation from Europe was superior to the three ancient ones that they had long been dealing with.

The historical discourse today points to this period as a time when European commercial empires became dominant. It describes them as the first steps in the march of industrial capitalism, a revolutionary force that changed the course of world history. At its core is the view that modern civilisation was born at the end of the 15th century and the next three centuries constituted something that might be called "early modern". No doubt this is credible when seen from Western Europe and when describing what was happening there. It is less compelling in relation to our region where the four civilisations were interacting, and regarded as equally important in the "Age of Commerce".

If we look at each of the civilisations during these centuries, there is an important corrective to the Eurocentric discourse. As described in my first lecture, Indic civilisation was the most attractive to both mainland and archipelagic parts of our region and left an indelible mark on the cultures developed there by most of its peoples. Later trading developments brought the region close to a Sinic-cum-Indic Buddhist civilisation and then to the Islamic half of Mediterranean civilisation that came by sea. The region remained open and inclusive and seemed to have been satisfied with selected bits of all three civilisations that they had incorporated into their own cultures.

But what was happening within these three civilisations? Each in its own way had been oriented towards the Eurasian core when it emerged in historical records. This can be seen in how each civilisation was vulnerable to attacks from the warring nomadic tribes of Central Asia, with the Indo-European speakers moving southwards and westwards and the Turko-

Mongolic conquering regions to their east, south and west wherever they had opportunities to do so.

For all these aggressors, and for the civilisations that they attacked or adopted, there were no ideas about borders. The battles fought were between those whose cultures were based on great mobility and the settled civilisations that fiercely defended the values and institutions they were proud of. Over the centuries, each of the ancient civilisations had survived many invasions. In contrast, when the Atlantic maritime powers arrived in Asia, they changed the range and quality of all trade, and the civilisations (Indic, Sinic and Islamic) involved seemed content to interact as peacefully as possible. The records show that the major conflicts were those between the European powers themselves, first the Dutch and Portuguese, at times the English and Dutch, and later the British and French.

In the meantime, back in Europe, a more fundamental struggle was going on. The thought leaders in several countries sought a better understanding of their common civilisation's ancient roots, not only to purify and reinvigorate their monotheistic faith but also to challenge traditional power structures within the Catholic Church. They sought to find a higher truth that went beyond inherited sacral values. It would be one based on scientific ideas and methodologies bringing about the material progress that proved their civilisation's superiority.

Thus began the rational and scientific quest for knowledge that would bring enlightenment to most Europeans. From the 17th to the early 18th centuries, they moved from a profound faith in the ancient to an affirmation of a humanistic modern. That led them to a secular willingness to learn everything they could about the world they encountered elsewhere, notably the American continents that was all theirs to conquer and civilise. The targets of the new mindset of discovery and exploration also included the ancient texts of the Indic and Sinic civilisations. Sanskrit studies in particular led them to see a common ancestral connection with other speakers of

Indo-European languages and their heritage of related cultures. For the British advancing into Mughal India, that also required them to study the deep historical linkages that connected the ancient Indo-European peoples with what later became Islamic Central Eurasia.[6]

In addition, the reports by Catholic missions introduced Western Europe to a somewhat idealised Sinic civilisation. The reports described the Confucian classics that provided moral guidance to the work of mandarins, chosen by merit via an elaborate examination system. The literati class there had produced comprehensive sets of historical and administrative records that focused on the value of order and harmony. There was also an emphasis on material well-being as the goal of good governance, and even the rights of imperial subjects to rebel and seek a new Mandate of Heaven if those standards were not met.[7]

In short, the peoples in Europe saw their world changing in unexpected ways. Although the changes in mindset had begun with Renaissance Italy, the earlier Islamic challenges during the Abbasid caliphate had included the growth of rational thought. The idea that the centres of learning could be exempt from the control of political authorities might also have induced the establishment of independent universities.

In any case, by the 18th century, two generations of philosophers had questioned the belief that humans had been wiser and morally purer in earlier times. The Protestant Christians had gone far from Catholicism to claim that individuals could choose to be better people by seeking God's help without certain intermediaries. In addition, the increasing ability to gain insight into the laws of nature encouraged scientific thinking, and more people began to believe that our capacity to reason could lead us to improve our understanding of the universe. That was a step towards a new civilisation in which history could help believers to appreciate God's will

---

[6] The Mughal Empire was a Muslim empire controlling much of South Asia, including India.

[7] "Mandate of Heaven" or *Tianming* was a Chinese political philosophy that rulers must be just in order to keep the approval of the gods.

and prove that advances to the human condition came from scientific knowledge and creative reasoning. In particular, historical research applied to biblical and other "oriental" textual studies together with the advances in the study of archaeology had extended our human capacity to better understand our fate.

All this also stimulated fresh thinking about the effectiveness of aristocratic rule. The new class of bourgeoisie behind the capitalist industries that were emerging led to a growing scepticism about tradition, especially the traditions that conferred immense power on the Church and on monarchy. Beginning with the Protestant movement against the Catholic Church and the scientific revolution against received wisdom, it was inevitable that the modern would challenge the ancient and bring forth the idea of progress.

Towards a New Frontier

The idea that civilised people had to deal with the uncivilised or the barbaric was common to many parts of the world. In ancient times, the three ways the civilised dealt with the barbaric were simple. They could drive barbaric peoples away as far as possible, as the Sinic Chinese tried to do on their long continental frontiers. Or they could defend their borders to keep the barbarians out, as both the Indic and Sinic civilisation were able to do most of the time. Or they could set out to make the barbarians civilised either by force or by example, as first the Islamic and then the Euro-Christian succeeded in doing in Asia.

However, the idea that modern civilisation could go further and bring progress to humankind without any divine intervention was new. The development of civilisation became a subject for serious study and fierce debates during the 18th century. Ancient civilisations were identified and research was done to show why most of them did not survive and had to give way to something better. Studies also explained why some regions did not produce their own civilisations, but developed distinctive local cultures by learning from one another and from neighbouring civilisations. These local cultures could, after sovereign nations were developed, become the bases for national cultures.

By the end of the 18th century, many thought leaders in Western Europe saw that a modern civilisation could transform the ancient ones. With a successful Enlightenment project, the time would come when there is only modern civilisation. As a progressive force, it would improve the human condition by creating a rich and powerful world in which there is only a single global civilisation in place of all ancient civilisations. Everyone in the world would then enjoy the same kind of life that the advanced modern nations have been enjoying.

Looking back from that vision of the future, we can see different examples of what had happened in history when any two civilisations came into contact. For example, in the case of the Indic and the Sinic, the impact was all one-way when Buddhism became an integral part of a culturally enriched Sinic civilisation, whereas the Sinic had no effect on the Indic whatsoever.

Another example was where kingdoms or empires fought one another in the name of civilisational differences of culture and ideology, like when a monotheistic faith had led the way to a revolutionary new civilisation. This was when the persecuted Hebrews and Christians prevailed, and their faith in a single God became embodied in an imperial Greco-Roman hegemony whether orthodox or papal. Then followed the Islamic Arab challenge that offered what was seen as a purer route to seek God's truth. After intense struggles for supremacy, their conflict spread across long distances to confront the heathen or pagan faiths both on land and at sea. Both believed that it was only a matter of time before all cultures would see the light.

With that background of civilisational effect in mind, we can see how transformative the revolutions in Europe were. They were not only scientific, philosophical, capitalist and technological but also had a great impact on the political structures and dynamics of the time. At its most dramatic, the

English led the way with the execution of the absolutist King Charles I, with Cromwell's Commonwealth and with the ideas of Hobbes and Locke. These ideas were further radicalised to include the newly enlightened, including those of the French philosophers Voltaire, Rousseau and Diderot. And in a different context, their ideas turned into another kind of political revolution by a group of transatlantic Englishmen in New England, Pennsylvania, Virginia and New York. The meeting of minds there created a nation of citizens in the 13 colonies of the United States that was then followed by that of the Republic of France.

I shall take on the outcome of these revolutions in my next lecture. Before I end, let me suggest how Singapore and its neighbourhood was becoming the frontier zone of the two kinds of power that stood for Europe's modern civilisation in Asia. One was Bourbon France supporting a state-centred economy, and the other was the English and Dutch East India Companies backed by parliaments committed to free trade. Their rivalry in the Indian Ocean was intense and ended with British victory. The French

Figure 8. The French Revolution

Source: "The French Revolution" by tonynetone. This image is licensed under CC BY 2.0.

Revolution that followed overthrew the monarchy. In the words of Mallet du Pan, the revolution "devoured its children", and could be ultimately seen as futile. The revolution, which effectively removed the monarchy, paved the way for Napoleon Bonaparte to mount the series of military campaigns that demonstrated the power of a new national empire.

What did our region know about the imperial ideas that this new modern nation represented? The allies of the French in India would have known about the revolution. The Javanese, Bugis and Chinese working with the disintegrating Dutch East India Company should have been aware that the Dutch homeland was in danger. The few people in mainland Southeast Asia working with Catholic priests might have been aware that a civilisational renewal of some kind was taking place. Chinese mandarins dealing with the Portuguese in Macao and with the British and Dutch missions seeking official relations with Emperor Qianlong seemed to have sensed that major changes were afoot in Europe. What was certain was that none in our region and the neighbouring countries of India and China would have thought that those faraway events could become central to the future of their civilisations and cultures.

By this time, the British were masters of the Indian Ocean. With a base in Penang to assist their trade with China, they were quick to keep Dutch Malacca out of the hands of the French. When the Dutch company was disbanded and its state threatened by Napoleon, Lord Minto in Calcutta appointed one Stamford Raffles to Java as Lieutenant Governor. That could be seen as the first move towards bringing modern civilisation to the island of Singapore a decade later. A new kind of empire was being launched. I shall take up that story in the next two lectures.

Question-and-Answer Session
Moderated by Dr Norshahril Saat

Dr Norshahril Saat: Thank you, Prof Wang, for that very insightful lecture. As we all know, this is the second part of his four-part lecture series. In Lecture I, Prof Wang spoke about the relationship between cultures and civilisation, particularly how Southeast Asian communities engage with Indic, Sinic and Islamic civilisations. It's interesting to observe how civilisations elicited responses from local communities by way of strengthening and transforming their cultures. In today's lecture, Prof Wang again reiterated the point that the people in the region shared a remarkable confidence in their ability to define local identities that enabled them to interact with neighbouring civilisations.

Before we begin the question-and-answer session, I want to share some points from his sharing that struck me. Prof Wang began his lecture by looking at how the 13th century was pivotal because of Sinic and Islamic civilisations, and how they made their presence greater in this region. Prof Wang also made the distinction between the behaviour of mainland and archipelagic communities in Southeast Asia. Just to quote Prof Wang, "they each chose what they thought would enhance their quality of life and make their respective local cultures stronger and more distinctive". Today I think Prof Wang developed this argument further — he spoke about the impact of these interactions on local and national cultures. Prof Wang's lecture then moved into the "Age of Commerce" in the 18th century, often called the fourth civilisation. This is remarkable because this is when Christianity began to make further inroads into this region and competed with the Islamic half. He also demonstrated the extent of the impact of these civilisations and their rivalry in this region.

And of course, it's very interesting that Prof Wang made a distinction between the responses of the archipelagic communities, which are seen as more open as compared to the mainland communities. This actually elicited some thinking on my part because I was looking at Islamic communities and how they differ in terms of the Islamic orientation. Till today, we can see these differences between the coastal communities and the mainland communities. As such, I think we see a similar pattern happening both today and during the 18th century.

Towards the end of Prof Wang's lecture, he also covered the influence of capitalism, which is personally my favourite part of the lecture. I was interested in looking at colonial knowledge, the role of orientalism and how Europeans created the myth of the native in our region. I think Prof Wang also pointed out a shift in focus among these European powers particularly because of the intra-European rivalry among the Dutch, Portuguese as well as the English, and we can see that there was a greater emphasis on the more commercial and capitalistic aspects of colonisation. There was also a shift in terms of the discourse that looked at more of the indigenous tags and humanistic order in this region. These are some of the observations that I made that really struck me. Of course, there are many other takeaways from Prof Wang's lecture, but I think in the interest of time, let's move straight into the question-and-answer session.

Participant: The underlying tone of this Fellowship is on governance and you profess that you will deal with history in this lecture series. I thought there could be a synergy between governance and history. When I look back at Dr Goh Keng Swee's Harry G. Johnson Memorial Lecture in 1983 on economic development and the Singapore model of public administration, the centrepiece was Singapore's style of governance, but he had a very interesting point on the cultural, societal and historical part of it. He introduced the idea of the committed process of governance and the role of the young populist in society. He also cited that in the Meiji Restoration, it was the young who led this change. When one looks at contemporary Asia, there is the beginning of youths coming into socio-economic discourse. For example, in Malaysia, there is Mr Syed Saddiq, who is a minister at 25 years old. Mr Lee Kuan Yew and the first generation of the People's Action Party were also young people who, in two to three generations, had brought us from third world to first. What is your take on this?

Prof Wang Gungwu: I'm not sure how to link it up with what I've said so far. Let me say that when you talk about young people, I'm reminded of the story of Genghis Khan, how young he was when he got on his horse and led his people to conquer the world. So youths could be counted on, all the way back to the time when they were riding horses across the plains and conquering the world.

I think if you look at that early period, all those people who were conquerors, such as Alexander the Great, he had conquered a large part of what was the civilised world when he was very young. In his case, he died very young, so he achieved everything and then died in his 30s. I think he died even younger than when Mr Lee Kuan Yew became the Prime Minister of Singapore. And so I'm not sure age is that crucial, and it does depend on the culture and the timing. In those days, people didn't live that long. If you hadn't saved the world by 50, you weren't worth talking about. Today, we can still hope to start at 50. So today we have an advantage — we're given much more time. But I'm also not sure that you can do things any better just because you're older.

What I do find interesting about your point is that when someone like Goh Keng Swee talks about his generation and the governance involved, what they were referring to was already modern. I think Singapore was modern from the day Stamford Raffles arrived, unlike the rest of Asia where people had to learn about what modernity was, how to modernise and how to learn about the modern Western world. When Lord Minto sent Raffles here to Singapore, what the British brought, especially after the Anglo-Dutch Treaty by which the position of Singapore was clearly separated, was a structure of government based on the most modern ideas about government that was available in the West. This was according to what was set up by the East India Company and what was available in London or Calcutta, where the British was governing from. From day one, Singapore started as a modern port serving as a link in a chain of ports in the British Empire, which at that time was the most modern national empire in the world because their naval power reached all corners of the globe.

So Singapore actually had a very interesting start that none of our neighbours had. You could say Penang also had a similar start, but Penang was replaced by Singapore, which had a superior location at the foot of the peninsula that was open to the South China Sea. Singapore followed through, right down to 1965 where it became something quite different. So the modernity of Singapore started on day one, as I see it. What we're talking about is that Singapore was modern from day one.

Of all the *merantau* people who gathered in Singapore, some of them made their homes here and decided to settle.[8] And all these people were representing different civilisations. They were not part of that modern civilisation brought by the British. That modernity was centred in the structure of governance. However, the people's lives, the way they traded, the religions that they brought with them and so on, these were still part of different civilisations. In the eyes of the modern, these would be considered as part of ancient civilisations. What was happening was, as I suggested, our region was a place where these people brought with them their own religions, civilisations. And among them were the people who were native to the region who were very confident in their own local cultures.

These local cultures knew how to pick and choose from the civilisations that they were in contact with to make their cultures stronger and more

---

[8] *Merantau* refers to a kind of wandering, without a known destination. Although these wanderers initially expect to return home, many of them eventually make a commitment to another land, where they start a new life. The term was first used in Lecture I.

enriched. They were also not particularly alarmed by the fact that there were different cultures among them. The British Government in Singapore also did not try to change this. They were very practical and did the minimum necessary to make the port function. As such, the focus was on making the free port conditions attractive to people who could then help Singapore develop. The British had clear and simple objectives, and did not set up a very elaborate governance to achieve this. They recognised from very early on that the people were *merantau* and originated from different civilisations. Thus, they followed local practice and minimised the possibility of local conflict by allotting different parts of the island to the *merantau* and keeping their civilisations apart.

You can see that from the beginning, they had an instinctive understanding of an emerging plural society, although the idea of a "plural society" was not originally applied to Singapore. The phrase was actually used by Furnivall in the 20th century to describe the Dutch East Indies or present-day Indonesia.[9] But the idea of a plural society — which means that each community has their own sense of civilisation — was identified by the British. They recognised the individual groups as different and respected their differences. In that sense, Singapore started with a modern government recognising the civilisational differences among people.

Each of them was not necessarily local. They came from India, China and elsewhere, representing different civilisations — but they were all accustomed to living with one another and working with one another, without finding any great difficulty in doing so. This modern government from Raffles onwards recognised that they did not have to do much with these different groups of people. All they had to do was to provide a framework in which they could all function. As they functioned in their own civilisational context, intercultural disputes were minimal. By making trade and intercourse relatively harmonious, it was actually profiting the free port of Singapore.

---

[9] John Sydenham Furnivall was a British-born colonial officer and writer who lived in Burma.

From what I just shared, the idea of "modern" does not necessarily refer to managing and intervening in other people's practices. Modernity can be a kind of understanding of how to make the best use of the resources available. I think this modern attitude continued through the whole of Singapore's history down to its independence in 1965. Already in 1965 when Singapore started to become a nation (and I have to say it is still work in progress). It had started with that established base. A modern state was already there, they just continued with it and they continued to recognise that there were layers of civilisations in a plural society which they acknowledged as being legitimate, equal and essential for the order and harmony that the new nation needed. I'm sorry I didn't quite answer your question but that's how I would respond.

Participant: I want to ask a question in relation to Xi Jinping pushing the Chinese Dream and the great rejuvenation of the Chinese nation. China is also pushing the global Belt and Road Initiative. In your opinion, what are the implications of those initiatives on ASEAN and especially on Singapore in terms of culture and civilisation?

Prof Wang: I guess you're very impatient for me to get to the present. I understand the interest, so let me try and put it this way — I will simply say that China had its ancient civilisation threatened, and at the beginning of the 20th century, there were many Chinese leaders and intellectuals who thought that their civilisation had come to an end and that they needed to have a revolution. In fact, they had two revolutions — one in 1911 and the other in 1949. They needed two revolutions to modernise as they thought that otherwise, the civilisation and the country, China itself, would disappear. As such, the need to modernise was very urgent and they looked at it as absolutely essential to survive.

However, they modernised in very different ways from other civilisations. Among the Chinese themselves, they could not agree on how to modernise because what is modern is actually not so straightforward. It's not as simple as essentially a difference between the modern and traditional. The process of modernising is not as clear-cut as the modern pushing aside all traditions — not to depend on traditional practices for new developments but to use new methods of scientific research and technology to achieve more beneficial results for humanity. That was one drive, and one way to look at modernity, but in order to do that, you had to get rid of traditions. That was seen to have been done within the European civilisation itself. They did it by in fact pushing aside their own ancient traditions in certain areas in order to achieve modernity.

But let's go back to the example of China. For China, to forget their traditions was to completely turn away from the Chinese civilisation. There are people who accuse the generation involved in the May Fourth Movement of having gone too far to completely start afresh, and some say that they even invented the Chinese phrase *quanpan xihua* (全盘西化) that was used to mean total westernisation. Some believed that to be modern, you needed to get rid of all traditions. That was what they thought the Europeans did. But the Europeans did not really do all that. The Europeans did that only for certain things. They actually kept their Christian mission which carried all the values about what is good for humanity, what explains the universe and what makes our life meaningful. All those were carried in the civilisation, except that they were secularised. They turned those values from just a church mission into a scientific social mission for all humanity. It is important to note that they were doing it within their own traditions initially.

But for the Chinese to turn away from traditions altogether and totally start with *quanpan xihua* was unnecessary, and it also did tremendous damage to the confidence of the Chinese people. In the end they lost their way. In trying to do that, they were in fact caught between two major contradictory choices. One was to be more and more nationalistic — to save the country against foreigners. The other was to be revolutionary — to destroy all traditions and start afresh with no traditions whatsoever. I'm giving you two extreme examples, but you can see the Chinese dilemma at that time. Once you took the line that it was important to modernise by learning from the West, they found that the West was very complicated. For example, there was a West that was represented by liberal capitalism, and a West that was represented by varieties of socialism.

But in the Chinese context, as you know from modern Chinese history, they had to make a choice. This is why the young generation had to choose between the two political camps — the Kuomintang (KMT) and the Chinese Communist Party (CCP). Those who chose nationalism followed Sun Yat-sen and the KMT, and those who chose socialism followed the CCP and the Soviet Union model. However, both of these political units were modernising in two very different ways. Now I could go on about that but you can see that your question is very different from what I'm talking about at this stage. If you're patient enough to come to my last lecture, I will elaborate more on this.

Dr Norshahril: I promised to take one question online. The question is about the influence of language. You spoke about culture and the resilience of culture, but where does language feature in this? Language has a strong influence on one's values and cultural traditions, and when we look at contemporary Singapore today, we have the example of the Mother Tongue Language programme and how it shapes our cultural identity. Where do you see the role of language here and of course in dealing with the influences from the region?

Prof Wang: In my last session, I was also asked a question about language and I think my answer is still roughly the same, with regard to language and the transmission of culture. To start off, we must distinguish between language as a natural expression of human beings, and language as a literate language. Spoken language is natural and everybody has a different spoken language. Every little group has a different language that is peculiar to their group and as long as you communicate within your group, that language is functional. However, when we talk about civilisations, it is a literate language we are referring to, and literacy represents a different dimension of our human lives and our cultural existence. It carries memory — all the achievements that have been made in the past can be transmitted for generation after generation and can continue to be enriched and improved upon, and this also makes such languages borderless. When a language is literate, anybody can learn it and the knowledge it transmits.

On the other hand, a spoken language is something that is absolutely essential for cultures, and it's inward-looking within each group. Spoken languages are very deeply associated with one's whole life — it is deeply embedded in us all and that is something peculiar to every individual, their family and their close community.

Maybe the next question to be asked is in what ways do we distinguish between a spoken language and a literate language? Both are important but they're important on a very different scale. To me, without a literate language, you cannot transmit civilisations. There are many so-called ancient civilisations that the late historian Arnold Toynbee had identified, which I find difficult to agree with as they do not have a literate language of their own. They managed to develop a very sophisticated set of cultural traditions and heritage without actually having a literate language. I find it difficult to call such examples civilisations. I'd say those are very rich cultures, especially in Latin America, where they were able to produce fantastic cultures and had spoken languages but never had literacy. They were quite happy to take other people's languages and use other scripts to express themselves.

My last point is that there are many layers of sophistication in language too. In fact, you can use the literate language to measure the sophistication of your civilisation through what can be expressed. For example, the kind of language used by scientists and technologists today express a whole range of things that I don't understand at all. Language is used and I can read it, but I don't understand what is being expressed. Some of these terms and language can be almost impossible to understand unless you specialise in the field. I don't know if that makes the civilisation using such specialised language greater or better, but they do represent a different civilisational dimension that we have to consider.

Participant: The impression I have from your lecture is that technology emerged as something that was not very important when it came to civilisational power. I'm struck that it is in contrast with how one would approach the competition between major powers today, which is very often framed with technology as the paramount factor of competition. Is technology actually subordinate to the wider characteristics of civilisational power, such as governance and religion?

Prof Wang: That is a very big question indeed. If I may use my historian's privilege to answer it, technology has always been important in any group of people hoping to achieve a sense of superiority over somebody else. For example, the civilisation that could grow plants quicker or have better-quality wheat or rice has a superior technology to those who have very primitive agricultural instruments. So, in this sense, technology has always been important. Technology has been built into the way human beings developed over the millennia, so it's part of culture and civilisation.

Technology has never been out of play. In fact, if you're familiar with *Science and Civilisation in China* by Joseph Needham, he uses the words "science" and "civilisation", but of course the whole debate about science in China was that it was not really science as we understand it. It was actually technology. From the very beginning, the superiority of Chinese civilisation in the region was its superior agricultural technology. It enabled those areas down the two river valleys (the Yellow River and the Yangtze River) to produce agriculturally and enabled China to eventually become one of the richest empires in the world. This of course could also be observed in the Nile or Tigris-Euphrates.

So from that point of view, it's never been science, and it should be seen as technology. The technology and skills that human beings develop in order to do things better and improve their livelihoods are deeply rooted in the way civilisations and cultures grew. So if you compare the three civilisations (Indic, Sinic and Islamic) in this part of the world, the most important Chinese contribution has always been in the area of trade and technology. Sinic civilisation has not been very influential in ideational or political influences, which are very strong from India, and later on, Islam and Christianity were also strong in India. The Chinese have not had such ideational influence except on Vietnam. However, their influence on skills, manufacturing and technologies down to the present is still a strength of their civilisation.

Participant: With regard to the Nusantara archipelagic region, there is a version of history that posits that the Sri Vijaya civilisation was much more open and trade-oriented than Majapahit in Java. How do you account for that difference within the same Indic civilisation despite the fact that they share the same open maritime geography?

Prof Wang: This is a very interesting question. It came up in the last lecture's question-and-answer session as well. I don't think we should talk about Sri Vijaya civilisation or Majapahit civilisation. They are both part and parcel of Indic civilisation, but they have been localised and domesticated with specific indigenous elements. In the case of Sri Vijaya, it is more maritime-oriented because its political system was based on controlling sea routes and individual ports. On the other hand, the system of the Majapahit Empire (which came much later) was based on essentially an agrarian civilisation in East Java. As I previously said, though I'm not able to prove it, the fertility of the volcanic soil in Java enabled agriculture to be fantastically successful from the very beginning, whereas the islands in the rest of Nusantara had soil that was not fit for agriculture.

I am reminded of this story. Someone told me that the Javanese were such great peasants and fantastically successful with agriculture, that the Dutch wanted to bring their techniques to South Sumatra, Borneo and so on, but agriculture did not succeed in these places. Farming was tremendously difficult in those areas because the conditions were not at all like what they were in Java. So the agrarian basis for the Majapahit world, its political world and system of governance are all land-based. And this is reflected in the monuments of Borobudur, Prambanan and so on. We don't see anything like that in the rest of Nusantara because they were not interested in those kinds of monuments. They were interested in their mobility at sea and that was their strength. Incidentally, both these views are equally Indic. One was a little bit more Hindu (Majapahit) and the other (Sri Vijaya) was almost purely Buddhist. Sri Vijaya was very much the centre of Buddhist culture and the Chinese used Sri Vijaya to prepare themselves to study Buddhism on their way to India. I hope that answers your question.

Dr Norshahril: I think I would like to raise the final online question. You have spoken about the Indic (under which includes Hinduism and Buddhism), Islamic and Christian civilisations coming to our region, but what about other religions and beliefs not covered under these civilisations? Why did they not make as much inroad in our region? The examples given are Taoism and Confucianism. Do you have any thoughts on that?

Prof Wang: Confucianism and Taoism are part and parcel of what we know as Sinic civilisation. In fact, I would say that Sinic civilisation was greatly enriched by Buddhism, which came from India; so without that Indic component in Chinese civilisation, Chinese civilisation would be much poorer. Confucianism and Taoism were indigenous to Sinic civilisation, but Buddhism was from Indic civilisation. These together are the basis of

Sinic civilisation and this also actually underlines the point that I've been making — that civilisations are borderless. Anybody can borrow from these civilisations to make themselves better. Civilisations are different from cultures, in that cultures are localised and so they produce one's identity and sense of belonging. In comparison, civilisations don't have that. They actually can spread.

I don't know about any ancient religion that has survived to this day. For example, there was Zoroastrianism and Manichaeism in the old Iranian world. They lasted a long time but they have not survived today, and they have been absorbed in one way or another. There are still some people from these religions left — the Parsees (an adherent of Zoroastrianism) and some Zoroastrians are still around, but they are a very small group of people. That's a choice within the civilisation itself. It does not have an impact on the rest of the world today because of the small group size.

But look at the remarkable example of Hebrew and the Jewish people. They did not enlarge themselves in numbers, and were extremely exclusive. For a long time, nobody could become a Jew. At its strictest, you had to have a mother who was a Jew in order to be a Jew. Yet they have survived all this time, and some claim they were the source of inspiration for two civilisations — what became an Islamic civilisation and what became a Christian civilisation.

It is interesting that in spite of that, they remained completely identified with a very small group of people. They were not a civilisation almost by choice because they didn't believe that it was their job to spread their ideologies and influence. It was enough for them to be a "Hebrew nation". In fact, some people may argue that the first ancient nation was probably the Jewish nation because they had a sense of nationhood. That had a religious base, although it was not dependent on acquiring other national or civilisational characteristics. They were self-sufficient, to give a very narrow view.

Many old religions and civilisations change over time, while retaining certain identifying characteristics. I remember being fascinated to discover in the middle of Fujian, an old temple that claimed to be a Manichaean Temple, descended from an ancient civilisation originating in Persia and Iran. I have no doubt it's true, but it no longer looks anything like what we consider to be Zoroastrian or Manichaean. It looked very much like a Chinese temple to me. But the people there say they are descended from a group of believers from the Tang dynasty who had brought their civilisation to China. Only fairly recently during the Ming and Qing dynasty did their temple begin to be more like a Buddhist or Taoist one. But they never lost their sense of identifying with that ancient Middle Eastern civilisation.

As such, civilisations can develop and change over time, but as I said, they could also survive unchanged for a long time. An example is the Jews of Kaifeng. We don't know exactly when this group first arrived, but we know that the Jews arrived during the Tang dynasty from the 7th century onwards and possibly earlier. We know that they were trading in China and one group of them survived in Kaifeng. It's very difficult to explain why they didn't recognise themselves as Jews but their practices were mostly copied from what the Jewish people left behind. They all look Chinese because they intermarried with other Chinese over the centuries. It was later scholarly Catholic priests who discovered that they were descended from Jewish merchants who settled in Kaifeng a thousand years ago. In this case, we don't identify this Jewish community with any civilisation because they never transmitted practices and ideas to anybody else. They just kept their practices to themselves. And they are still following certain rituals that were practised only by the Jews, and which have been identified as such by scholars. These are some very interesting examples.

Dr Norshahril: Thank you, Prof Wang. I think we have to draw this question-and-answer session to a close. There are many points that were raised today that left me thinking. There are a number of works out there that describe the rise and fall of civilisations. Francis Fukuyama himself has written extensive volumes about this. But I think Prof Wang has shared something new and I've learned a lot talking about the interaction between civilisations and cultures. To me, the case study on Southeast Asia is particularly fascinating. There are no civilisations here per se, but of course, the interactions and the developments of local cultures are very interesting. Ladies and gentlemen, thank you very much and let's put our hands together to thank Prof Wang.

Lecture III
ENLIGHTENED MODERN

LECTURE III

In my last lecture, I referred to two revolutions in the 18th century that changed the course of history. Both were part of the Enlightenment civilisation that had earlier been identified as Christian European. Both revolutions were the products of reason and humanism that had undermined church authority and the credibility of feudal and dynastic empires. One strand turned decisively away from tradition and demanded critical rethinking about all transmitted knowledge. It placed its faith in scientific discovery and financial innovation in order that mankind could seek progress. It was time for the modern mind to strive to shape a superior civilisation. The other challenged the idea that power should rest with kings and nobles who had become obstacles to social progress. The citizenry was encouraged to establish new political structures that would enable them to build a new kind of state. That would provide the framework that would determine and protect their national culture and identity.

How each of the revolutions occurred and what made them successful has been the subject of innumerable studies. One set of writings stressed the ideals that galvanised these modernists to share their knowledge and scientific methods with all those willing and capable. The price to pay would be that they set aside the values and traditions that stood in the way of promised material progress. The other set of studies focused on the power enabling national empires to use this civilisation to bring radical changes in global affairs.

What enabled the Western European nations in the 19th century to dominate every corner of the world? They did so largely by occupying territory and building extensive empires. With their control of ports, colonies and protectorates, they obtained the natural resources needed to develop industries and markets in which their manufactures could replace those that were locally made. By doing so, they saw themselves as modern and civilised — people ready to help the natives escape their ancient and

Figure 1. **The World: Colonial Possessions and Commercial Highways (1910)**

Source: Courtesy of the University of Texas Libraries, The University of Texas at Austin. Retrieved from https://maps.lib.utexas.edu/maps/historical/ward_1912/world_1910.jpg.

backward civilisations. From that perspective, what they did marked a turning point in world history.

Up to the 18th century, the four civilisations (Indic, Islamic, Sinic and Christian European) meeting in Asia were primarily focused on commercial rivalries in and between the territories that each could occupy and control. Where civilisational differences were concerned, the protagonists still displayed some measure of mutual respect. A century later, the national empires that came out of the Enlightenment were more judgemental. They set out to get rid of whatever they thought was backward and inefficient. That enabled them to insist that modern standards of civilisation should prevail in the lands under European control. The idea of the enlightened modernity and its histories are what I will address in this lecture.

National Empires

I had earlier described the multicultural dynastic empires with long histories in every civilisation. Several were resilient and still defending themselves down to the 20th century, notably the European Austro-Hungarian, the Tsarist Russian and the Islamic Ottoman in three continents (Asia, Europe and Africa), and the Sinic Qing in China. Each of these empires was identified with an ancient civilisation. The Indic was different in that it was not linked to a single empire, having had a subordinate relationship with the Islamic Mughal and then with the British national empire standing for modern civilisation.

The successful East India Companies of the 17th and 18th centuries had received greater royal naval support over time. As a result, when the time came to act in the name of the nation, commercial empires based on cities like London and Amsterdam laid the foundations of national empires. For example, the Dutch East India Company (VOC) was officially made a national entity following the Napoleonic wars. The English East India Company (EIC) lasted longer independently and officially, but was clearly a British national commitment by the time of the Opium Wars in China.

The company was totally taken over after the 1857 Indian Mutiny ended Mughal rule in India. The British Raj was a *national* triumph.

An illustration of how this affected our region was the international treaty signed by national empires that I mentioned in my last lecture. I refer to the Anglo-Dutch Treaty of 1824. It marked the national–imperial border along the Straits of Malacca that, over 120 years later, divided Malaysia and Indonesia into two modern nation-states. It is sobering to think that our region became part of one of the most powerful political constructs in history when national empires claimed to represent modern civilisation.

Thus developed the idea that the nation-state could harness the new Enlightenment civilisation in its enterprise to lead the world to progress. Their mission was not merely to expand power and wealth and take territory wherever that was available. It was also to bring modernity to the benighted races and put an end to the old empires still clinging to their feudal and dynastic ways. In the context of those civilisations that were still seen as ancient, the message was that the ancient needed to modernise or they could lose the right to be called civilised.

Inspired by the mission of civilising the lesser races and advancing the human condition, the national empires could then conduct wars of conquest as a progressive act. How they did so is on record and there are innumerable studies about what they achieved. More recently, there have been corrective writings that exposed the high price non-Europeans had to pay for that success. I shall not dwell here on the brutal and ugly side of that story. In order to advance their trading and territorial interests, all empires were at times prepared to be uncivilised if not downright barbaric. The difference was that the European empires in the 19th and 20th centuries imagined that they were doing so to advance modern civilisation.

The idea of the nation-state was soon connected to the innovations of the Industrial Revolution and imperial capitalism. This was also when France became a republic and was projected as an empire abroad. Napoleon might have seen himself as a modern leader fighting in the name of freedom, equality and fraternity. But as the emperor of the French nation, he was identified within Europe as a serious threat to the older dynastic empires. This forced the majority of "ancient regimes" to unite against him.

After Napoleon was defeated and the Congress of Vienna redrew the map of Europe, the monarchy was restored. The French nation now acted in the name of its emperors until it became a republic again. As a national empire, it did well in the Mediterranean and on the West African coast. They were less ambitious in the Indian Ocean where they had to accept a secondary role and played second fiddle to the powerful British navy. Together as empires representing modern civilisation, the British and the French then agreed to avoid fighting one another. When the whole world

Figure 2.   Napoleon Bonaparte

Source: "Austria-03330 — Napoleon I" by archer10 (Dennis). This image is licensed under CC BY-SA 2.0.

was for the taking, these empires should keep their competition civil and concentrate on the task of eliminating the ancient empires that offered any resistance.

The Anglo-Dutch Treaty marked a notable step towards acquiring territorial control wherever there was an opportunity to do so. The Dutch were left free to expand their empire systematically and they subjugated all the local rulers in Java, Sumatra and the rest of the Nusantara islands. The British pushed further inland beyond Bengal, Madras and Lower Burma, even venturing forth towards Nepal and the Tibetan borders. And the French were left to move actively from Cochin China to Cambodia and Annam.

For Southeast Asia and the new port of Singapore, the local leaders would have been aware that the Dutch forces, like the Portuguese and the Spanish before them, were weakening. They would have known that the British were in control of the Indian Ocean from Calcutta, Madras and Bombay. They might also have been aware that the main imperial rivals were monarchical Britain and Republican France. They would certainly have heard that the British had taken the Dutch lands in Ceylon and the strategic Cape Town settlement in South Africa. When the EIC Governor-General Lord Minto sent young 30-year-old Stamford Raffles to take control of Java, it showed how confident he was of British maritime supremacy.

Interacting With the Modern: The Indic

From the perspective of long-distance trade in Asia, European naval power had enabled modern capitalism to dominate our region. By the first decades of the 19th century, maritime Southeast Asia was largely in the hands of European national empires: the Philippine islands since the 17th, all the coastal areas of Islamic Nusantara by the 18th, followed by the southern coasts of the Malay Peninsula. It was clear that the Dutch and the British would share the maritime polities while the French were left to contest British advances on the Southeast Asian mainland. All three empires were aware that the region had distinct local cultures, and that these cultures were influenced by three ancient civilisations. The Indic was still mixed in with the dominant Islamic in the archipelago while the Indic-Buddhist was strong on the mainland. Then there was the Sinic state of Vietnam that also had a share of Indic and Islamic influences. Furthermore, there were numerous Sinic trading communities scattered in many parts of our region.

However, it is less clear whether our region's political leaders were aware that they were dealing with empires acting as missionaries for modern civilisation. The Buddhist kingdoms, Vietnam and Nusantara Islam were confident that their local cultures could meet the modern challenge and adapt accordingly as they had done in the past. Their leaders were also aware that other civilisations were responding elsewhere. They saw how the Hindu and the Islamic Mughal states of the subcontinent faced the advance of British power and how the Buddhist Siamese were dealing with French and British demands. They might also have been aware that Qing China and Tokugawa Japan had become more watchful of growing European power in their neighbourhood.

This was especially true of the reactions to the EIC's advances in Bengal. Men like Indian reformer Ram Mohan Roy of the early 19th century and his generation were prepared to examine afresh some traditional practices so that their civilisation could stand up to Western power and wealth. But that openness to heritage renewal was rare. There is little evidence of political reform among the Indian ruling classes elsewhere, although local protests in different parts of British India eventually did lead to efforts to modify the rigid caste system and remove whatever was identified as superstitious practice.

However, it was not until the beginning of the 20th century that the Indians who had lived and studied abroad began to discover the oneness of "India" as a civilisation and openly opposed the British Raj. Leaders like Tilak Maharaj and Mahatma Gandhi inspired a new generation of men like

Figure 3. Statue of Ram Mohan Roy in Front of Bristol Cathedral, College Green

Source: "Ram Mohan Roy (Dec2010)" by Matt Neale from UK. This image is licensed under CC BY-SA 2.0.

Jawaharlal Nehru, Mohd Jinnah and Subhas Chandra Bose to go beyond the literary and cultural achievements of Rabindranath Tagore and seek modern political renewal. Many of them found inspiration in the modern western schools they attended. They were conscious that most of these schools were established by European Christian missionaries arguably operating within imperial frameworks, but they were confident that their own wisdom classics were alive and would be able to lift them above mere imitations of the West.

In our region, it was known how the heartland of Indic civilisation had undergone internal power shifts that ended with the retreat of Buddhism

Figure 4.   Subhas Chandra Bose

Source: "Subhash Chandra Bose — Postcard Picture" by S.S. Brij Basi & Sons Karachi. This image is licensed under CC BY 4.0. This image has been cropped from the original.

except on the island of Ceylon. The reverse was true in mainland Southeast Asia where it was Buddhism that flourished with the fall of the Angkorian Empire. This marked a major divide in Indic civilisation. Remarkably, it came about without any disruption in relations with the Hindu states, with Hinduism considered so closely related to Buddhism. What was extraordinary was that, despite the way Indic civilisation had shared political, social and cultural power with the Hindu parts of the region for centuries, the permanent separation of Buddhism from the rest of Indic civilisation could not be avoided. The Buddhists thereafter monopolised political power in Sri Lanka and in the mainland kingdoms of the Irrawaddy, Menam and Mekong valleys but was almost totally rejected in its original home in India.

At the same time, it was remarkable how Indic civilisation was no less resilient even after its Buddhist limb was cut off. When Islamic forces invaded Northern and Central India, the Indic upper castes of Brahmin

Figure 5. Jama Masjid of Delhi, a Mosque Built by Mughal Emperor Shah Jahan

Source: "Jama Masjid, Delhi, India" by Peter Rivera. This image is licensed under CC BY 2.0.

and Kshatriya were able to deal successfully with their Muslim conquerors. Although there were some conversions to Islam, what was remarkable was the way Hindu civilisation remained intact. It survived not only in the communities under direct Muslim rule, but also as autonomous kingdoms like the Rajput and the Maratha that, when not fighting against further encroachment of their lands, made their peace with the Islamic empires.

Here was a civilisation that remained alive and vibrant though militarily and politically subdued by a younger civilisation, which came in the form of the British Empire. That experience showed that the Hindu leaders knew how to give way when that was necessary, and to take back whenever opportunities arose. When British power weakened Mughal imperial control, several states worked with the British to redefine their own interests. The British in turn seized every opportunity to establish the framework of a multilayered empire that was to be the Jewel in the British Crown. Men like James Mill in his history of British India were quick to condemn the ancient civilisation that the British had to live with. Thomas Macaulay's "Minute on Indian Education" went further to prescribe what he thought would civilise its people. But neither could determine what the Indians would do.[1] British officials and businessmen working on the ground soon realised how culturally secure the Indian peoples were and how well their elites could determine what they thought their people really needed.

Buddhist Indic

By the 19th century, the elites in Southeast Asia were aware that the competing Western empires each had their distinctive cultures with their own national version of modernity. The conquered kingdoms had little choice but to accept what was thrust upon them. For a region without its own civilisation, the peoples in our region continued to identify with their local cultures that each retained features of Indic and Islamic civilisation. Sinic civilisation had its presence through Chinese traders, later joined by their Japanese partners. Within the region, Vietnamese expansion down the peninsula came at the expense of the Muslim Chams and the Buddhist Khmers.

I mentioned that the common faith in Theravada Buddhism in the mainland states did not bring them unity. Burmese efforts to conquer Siam and the Siamese incursions into Cambodia underlined how strong local state cultures were. This was notably true when the Siamese retained their links with Qing China, while at the same time trading profitably with Britain and settling their eastern borders with French Indochina. Both Siam monarchs Rama IV and Rama V understood the Chinese and learnt to adapt to British and French variants of Enlightenment civilisation.

The Burmese kings also tried to go their own way. But having been involved in dealing with British advances among the local tribal minorities

---

[1] "Minute on Indian Education" (1935) was a speech given by British historian and politician Thomas Macaulay on the need to impart English education to the Indian people.

in Bengal, Manipur and Assam, it is hard to understand why they did not take note of how elites of Bengal had responded, how their leaders took the road to a famous cultural renaissance and tried to do something similar. Instead, they badly misjudged British power and chose to fight three wars and lost them all. The British concluded that their resistance was uncivilised and did not give them the choice of being a colony. Instead, to add insult to injury, Burma was made a province of India. Being part of British India did not bring them closer to their Indic civilisational roots. The British use of Indians in administering Burma made the Burmese even more conscious that their Theravada Buddhism had become something quite distinct from its civilisational roots.

The British made no mistake with the Straits Settlements that they governed from Calcutta. They brought with them both skilled and unskilled workers from Indic centres, notably from South India and Tamil Ceylon. But they kept good relations with Nusantara Islam and for commercial reasons continued to welcome Chinese traders, artisans and coolies to help develop the resources of the Malay Peninsula. It did not then matter when some local Indian leaders showed support for the *swaraj* or self-governance movement, and for the Greater India Society that highlighted Indian influence in the. region. This was so even though the British were aware that there was local admiration for some form of Pan-Asianism against Western dominance.

The British saw Indic civilisation as ancient and fragmented and no threat to their Enlightenment vision. What did take them by surprise was the 1915 Muslim Sepoy revolt in Singapore during World War I. It was a minor incident, but the mutineers were seen to have a civilisational link to the Ottoman caliphate that was allied to their German enemies. That was a reminder that our region had no clear western borders.

This was also true in the east where French advances northwards into Tongking (northern Vietnam) were opening the southern gates into China. The historical relations between Vietnam and Qing China pointed to Sinic civilisation as the last target of the European empires. For about 300 years, most trade was conducted via Macao and what was known about Sinic cultures was glimpsed through southern Chinese merchants. As mentioned earlier, Jesuit priests did reach Ming and Qing cultural centres but they had little success in winning over Chinese elites to a Catholic European worldview. They did better in Vietnam. The French civilising mission together with their imperial adventures helped to loosen Vietnam from the Sinic framework and eventually brought it closer to Southeast Asia.

As noted earlier, China had a very different relationship with the Europeans when they arrived. Lack of official interest in overseas trade meant that the Portuguese were allowed to monitor all foreign merchant arrivals. The founding Manchu emperors were watchful but not unduly concerned about European advances in our region. When Emperor Qianlong met Lord Macartney, he was aware that the British were gaining power in India, which was China's Buddhist "Western Heaven". But the emperor and his immediate successors had no inkling that before long that power, through two Opium Wars, would expose the vulnerabilities of China's civilisation.

The Islamic

As for the Islamic leaders in the archipelago, they were in touch with the Ottoman caliphate and the centres of education in Egypt and Arabia, and were aware that the Europeans claimed a superior modernity. They were aware of the intense questioning of received knowledge among Muslim thinkers in the Eastern Mediterranean, on both sides of the Persian Gulf, and in Northern India. And they would have known about the Wahhabism of Saudi Arabia, although its influence during the 19th century was uneven.[2] But they saw no concerted response to European expansion because the Muslim world seemed unafraid that its civilisation was in any danger.

Our region's Muslims shared that confidence. They were among the earliest to have been inspired by the Wahhabi call for a return to a purist faith. This was when the Padri movement in West Sumatra sought to cleanse

---

[2] Wahhabism is a Sunni Islamic fundamentalist movement originating from Najd, Arabia.

Minangkabau society of its local *adat* cultures, which forced the *adat* leaders to ask the Dutch for help.[3] And although the Java War of 1825 was a political rebellion against Dutch colonial rule, Prince Diponegoro was an early example of a leader motivated also by Islamic civilisational ideals. Neither of the revolts was successful. It was not until the latter half of the 19th century that Nusantara leaders began actively to join their Islamic brethren elsewhere in recognising that the changes taking place around them could undermine the foundations of their civilisation.

In the widespread Nusantara world, despite the strong base of Indic influences and the steady spread of the Islamic *Ummah* its open maritime environment left it with more choices and a willingness to deal with other civilisations with confidence. When I was editing an Asian historical monographs series, I recall being fascinated by the *Tuhfat al-Nafis* in which rich accounts of maritime politics in the old Johor Empire in Riau and the Malacca Straits demonstrated skills of the Bugis in handling Dutch and British company officials. They demonstrated confidence in their Islamic networks at the time when the VOC agents were notoriously corrupt and inefficient.

Nusantara Islam was Sunni with strong Sufi linkages, and had close ties with its Quranic teachers from India and the Arab world. Although distant and indirect, it kept regular connections with the caliphate. In its dealings with the Dutch and the British, it was represented by lively and distinctive local cultures that were recognisably Malay, Acehnese, Minangkabau, Sundanese, Javanese, Bugis and others. In their Islamic heritage, there was a consistent bond between its civilisation and the local cultures that it had enriched. And despite the challenges of modernisation, that relationship prevailed in every part of our archipelagic world.

The European national empires thus brought Enlightenment civilisation into a tense relationship with those in our region that had co-existed with

---

[3] "Adat" is a generic term derived from Arabic to describe a variety of local customary practices and traditions deemed compatible with Islam as observed by Muslim communities in the Balkans, North Caucasus, Central Asia and Southeast Asia.

one another for nearly 800 years. With their roots in the Greco-Roman classics, British scholars did learn to appreciate the Indo-Aryan base of the Indic civilisation. They also knew enough of their past involvements in their crusades in the Mediterranean not to unnecessarily antagonise the monotheistic Islamic conquerors that had preceded them in India. India during the 19th century thus demonstrated the viability of a tripartite set of relationships that showed how different civilisations were not confined by political borders. With cultural sensitivity and diplomatic skills, it was possible for national empires to accommodate more than one civilisation. They could live with different civilisations even though they had little sympathy for and limited understanding of the values that each represented.

The Sinic

While Anglo-French naval forces were reaching the Sinic world in the 1850s, two other imperial armies were pushing overland in northern Eurasia and the North American continent. Although moving in opposite directions, each did so with its own version of Christian civilisation. In Central Asia, the Russians dealt with Islamic peoples whose civilisation they had earlier been defending against for centuries. Now they were pushing eastwards and gaining control of the numerous khanates.[4] In addition, their Cossack adventurers were crossing beyond the Siberian steppes in ways that were comparable to the young Americans who were enjoined to go west and move the frontier towards the Pacific Ocean.[5] Both the United States (US) and Russia were engaged in territorial expansion among tribal peoples until they reached the shores of Alaska.

Although they were both sending colonists to their continental frontiers, theirs were different kinds of empire. The dynastic Russian had started early and by 1689 had reached the borders of Qing China and signed the first European treaty with a Sinic Empire. The Americans, on the other

---

[4] Khanates refer to regions ruled by a khan, a supreme Mongol or Turkic tribal leader.

[5] Cossacks were a people in southern Russia who became aggressive warriors (in the name of Russia) during the 16th and 17th centuries.

hand, arrived as citizens of a modern nation-state after they had freed themselves from the British Empire. Their overland expansions from opposite directions towards the Sinic world deserve attention because that prepared the way for their later roles in shaping the modern world.

During the 19th century, the Russians not only challenged British power in Central Asia, but also took lands from the Manchus and the Mongols. In comparison, the American navy alarmed Tokugawa Japan by sailing into Tokyo Bay. But it did not threaten the Japanese and took no lands. Instead, they were content to follow the British into China as capitalists and missionaries. The Qing Chinese were impressed by their entrepreneurial dynamism and thought that their presence could help them to modernise and resist the European national empires that came via Southeast Asia. It was not until the 20th century that the Americans and Russians were seen as offering rival versions of modernity and introduced the Chinese people to different revolutionary paths.

The Sinic civilisation that the British and French encountered was different from the Indic and the Islamic by having developed a centralised bureaucratic state that governed an agrarian empire for over 2,000 years. Its vision of a universal moral order of "all under Heaven" (*tianxia*) had emerged under ancient thinkers and teachers of the Zhou dynasty. As a unified dynastic empire, the civilisation was guided by Sinic values but not always under a Chinese ruling house. Its civilisational continuity was anchored in sets of classical texts and historical records in the Chinese language. This has, in succession, enabled the Mongol-ruled Yuan, the Han-ruled Ming and the Manchu-ruled Qing dynasties to be portrayed as equally Chinese. What was decisive was victory on the battlefield. That allowed any new dynastic claim to have received the Mandate of Heaven. That provided the civilisation with a deep-rooted state structure through which it could fall and rise again under a variety of rulers. While the state depended on its agrarian base, its conquerors could come from outside that base, from the desert and the steppes. Throughout history, none of the dynastic empires had been threatened by hostile forces coming by sea. None

Figure 6.   Framed Image of Sun Yat-sen in Beijing

Source: "Sun Yat Sen" by Dalee2200. This image is licensed under CC BY-SA 4.0.

had ever seen any danger to the civilisation resulting from mere naval defeats.

That heritage was challenged after 1840 when British victories off the China coast led to the Treaty of Nanking and the cession of Hong Kong. Thereafter, in the new European discourse, Qing China was identified as some kind of national empire where the Manchus ruled over Han, Mongol, Turkic Muslim and Tibetan peoples. This approach encouraged Han Chinese in the south to point to the Manchu as foreign conquerors who should be driven out of China. From the Taiping rebels who claimed to be "Christian" and captured most of South China, all the way to the English-educated Sun Yat-sen who led an anti-Manchu republican revolution, the first steps were taken towards the Enlightenment idea of a modern nation-state.

Later in the century, after being defeated by the Japanese navy in 1894 and following the "Eight Powers" from Europe lifting the Siege of Peking in 1900, the Qing Court was demoralised. The Manchu aristocracy could see that the end of their dynastic rule was near. They therefore agreed, after being guaranteed that their lives would be protected, that the Emperor Xuantong abdicate in favour of Yuan Shikai as President of the Republic of China. At this point, it could be said that the Manchu Qing did not represent Sinic civilisation and the new Republican successor state was neither an empire nor a nation. And except for a handful of overseas Chinese and the entrepreneurs in Hong Kong and the Treaty Ports, the Chinese literati class did not see themselves as modern.

The speed at which Chinese civilisation had fallen has been difficult to explain. In Angus Maddison's *The World Economy*, economic data suggests that the Qing China in 1820 had close to one-third of the world's

Figure 7. England During the Industrial Revolution

Source: Samuel Griffiths, "Guide to the Iron Trade of Great Britain," (1873), 110. Retrieved from: https://www.flickr.com/photos/internetarchivebookimages/14761790294/.

economy. By the early 1900s, it was below 10 per cent and fell further to slightly below 5 per cent in the 1970s.[6] The rise of capitalism and the Industrial Revolution certainly made a great difference to the global distribution of wealth. However, a civilisation's vitality is not only measured by a country's gross domestic product. More significant was whether others treated its values with respect. In that context, China's "century of humiliation" was not about naval defeats, but really about how Western reports described its people condescendingly as superstitious and ignorant and its ancient civilisation as backward if not barbaric.

Several studies have shown how China-watching in the West went from a degree of admiration to a mixture of pity and contempt during the 19th century. There was a distinction between the perspective of modern civilisation and that of imperial triumphalism. The Enlightenment West saw it as a duty to help China modernise while the national empires focused on the opportunities to maximise profit and political control at China's expense. The Chinese elites were also divided. At one end were those who railed against the self-proclaimed progressives who had lost faith in the classical heritage and were willing to imitate the West. At the other extreme were those who blamed everything on traditional leaders and accused the mandarin class of clinging blindly to past glories. The traditional literati elites had failed to recognise that the country had to learn from the advanced nations and that they had to do so as quickly as possible.

The fact that Sinic civilisation had been identified with an undivided dynastic state had been seen as a source of strength. That view was challenged when Meiji Japan decided to leave "the East" and look to "the West", and follow the path of modern Western empires. When this happened, it undermined China's civilisational claim to political superiority. About the same time, the French conquest of Vietnam drew that country away from China's orbit. After that, with Japan's control of first Korea and

---

[6] Angus Maddison, *The World Economy: Volume 1: A Millennial Perspective and Volume 2: Historical Statistics* (Paris: OECD Publishing, 2006), 263.

then Manchukuo, the ancient Sinic inter-state framework was dismantled. One can understand why, by the May Fourth generation, so many young Chinese believed that China had to become a nation in order to be modern and civilised.

Japan was an example of a country with a distinct culture that had taken what it wanted from a nearby civilisation that was both Sinic and Indic-Buddhist and had done so without losing its core cultural values. In a less distinct way, the peoples of Korea and Vietnam had also benefitted from selecting civilisational values from their larger neighbour, including the Indic-Buddhist civilisation that they all shared. All three developed national attributes that were enhanced by their willingness to learn from Sinic civilisation. When all three were exposed to Enlightenment modernity, they responded readily to the idea of national statehood. Japan can certainly be said to have led the way by proclaiming their national empire as modern and, as a result, made their distinctive contribution to the end of the European "Age of Empires".

Nations and Revolutions

It was Enlightenment civilisation that connected modernity with progress and paved the way for a world of nation-states. I shall not try to describe the development of the national empires of the 19th and 20th centuries. There are many studies of that phenomenon, including more recent ones that analysed the intense rivalries among them that led eventually to their destruction in two world wars. However, what enabled them to dominate the world, including the science and industrial capitalism that gave them so much wealth and power, and the rights of citizens that led them to ideals of freedom and quality, have remained to inspire the elites in Asia to seek that modernity for themselves.

What is interesting is how the peoples who had been subjugated by the national empires responded to nationhood, and how that turned the world against colonialism and imperialism. It was remarkable that the first generation of nationalist leaders in our region realised that, with the earlier layers of civilisations that had enriched their cultures, they could deal with this modernity from a strong local base.

The idea of becoming a nation is not new. It has an ancient history going back to when some sense of identity was shared by a multitude of tribes of common descent. Any group of people who had lived together for a long time could be described as a potential nation that shared a common culture. But the right of such nations to become sovereign states became possible only after the Treaty of Westphalia of 1648. The treaty was signed to enable empires, kingdoms and principalities to have their borders formally recognised and thereby end decades of brutal wars in Europe. The dynastic or feudal empires each consisted of ethnic groups that were, or could have been nations, but the empires continued to expand their territories even after the treaty was signed. It is misleading to confuse these sovereign states with the modern nation-states in which the whole citizenry constitutes the nation.

That emerged later in France and the US. The popular will expressed through a democracy with ideals that included liberty and equality provided the model for the nation-states of the 19th century. They focused on being based mainly on a common language, one religion and a shared history, and were sovereign states with recognised borders. That allowed their citizen politics to rise above the "divine right" claimed by dynastic rulers and enabled its nationals to share a common civilisation without conceding their own distinctive identity. Benedict Anderson may be right to call this identity one of "an imagined community". He was certainly correct when he used the term to describe the new nations of our region that were easier to imagine than to bring to fruition. In large parts of Europe, it took decades of war and civil wars and the dismantling of empires like the Hapsburg and Austro-Hungarian, the Tsarist Russian and the Ottoman before nation building could begin. And new nations have been redrawing borders and redefining themselves ever since.

After the defeat of Napoleon, the national ideal spread to monarchical Netherlands and the United Kingdom, Spain and Portugal, and the Scandinavian states. Then came the rise of Italy and Prussia after the 1848 revolutions and that of the German Empire following the defeat of Republican France in 1870. That impact on European politics pointed to the aggressive flaw in Enlightenment civilisation that proved fatal by lending support to two world wars. However, at the time, these events were primarily European affairs and had little effect on Southeast Asia.

What was significant to the world was the radicalisation of the working people who saw themselves as victims of industrial capitalism. They

Figure 8. Statue of President Mustafa Kemal Ataturk, the First President of Türkiye, in Artvin Valiliği

Source: "File: Artvin Ataturk monument 3990.jpg" by Dosseman. This image is licensed under CC BY-SA 4.0.

included artisans, factory labour and the peasantry whose livelihoods had become more precarious. Accompanied by an educated middle class demanding political participation, the growing social unrest led to the revolutions of 1848. The failure of the Chartists (those involved in the working-class movement from 1838 to 1857) in Britain and a variety of socialists and anarchists on the continent intensified the hostility against the plutocratic enemies of freedom and equality. They also inspired the followers of Karl Marx to formulate plans to organise class-based movements of a proletariat revolution.

The revolt against liberal capitalism went on to take different forms. By the 20th century, it produced the Bolshevik Revolution of 1917 in Russia, the mass movements of Fascism in Italy as well as Central and Eastern Europe and National Socialism in Germany. They were all part of the story of the different roads that modern nationalism had taken in Europe. I shall only touch on those parts that were connected to national empires and thereby the new nation-states that were created when those empires self-destructed.

It was the European Enlightenment that sowed the seeds of deadly internal conflict. The skills that were needed to develop industrial capitalism, and the scientific inventions that enhanced military power, could all be studied and learnt. When rival nation-states like Germany and Italy mastered comparable skills, there came the ambition to use them to build their own empire. Sooner or later, even while sharing the same civilisation, the British and French national empires felt the need to go to war to fight any new power that might challenge their supremacy.

The modernised German nation-state became strong in science and technology and acquired the capitalist urge for imperial expansion. This led the European civilisation to turn against itself in World War I. I shall not get into the complex reasons why this war might have been unavoidable. Perhaps Graham Allison was right about Britain and Germany falling into the Thucydides Trap, and Britain could not allow German power to rise further. It was clear that World War I between national empires claiming to be agents of civilisation ended unhappily for these first nation-states. It is also true that the failure to make good peace led to World War II. The Europeans had only themselves to blame for that. The League of Nations "to end all wars" was still dominated by national empires and therefore fatally flawed. Deadly rivalries among them were merely suspended with the dissatisfied protagonists gearing up for another war, and that led to the destruction of the national empires altogether. Needless to say, the end of World War II was good news to the peoples in their colonies and protectorates.

By the end of the 19th century, leaders in our region had become aware of the difference between the imperialist powers and the Enlightenment civilisation they had claimed to be bringing to a backward world. The great powers had used their superior weaponry to conquer territory and were prepared to destroy the lives of the races they considered to be inferior. But the people they dominated in our region had had their local cultures enriched by civilisations with deep roots and their elites had the capacity to study and learn from the conquerors. When they agreed to modernise as nation-states, they saw that they could choose from different parts of the Enlightenment civilisation that they encountered. It was not surprising that they would want to control their own fates and compete economically. In order to do that, they had to prove that they could learn from their masters

Figure 9. Flag of the League of Nations

Source: "File: Flag of the League of Nations (1939).svg" by Martin Grandjean. This image is licensed under CC BY-SA 4.0.

while preserving those parts of what they considered central to their new national identity.

In the Indic, Islamic and Sinic worlds, the elites were proud of their civilisations but were keen to modernise and "self-strengthen". They went abroad to study economic, administrative and managerial skills. They built modern schools and colleges. They also learnt to organise political parties with mass appeal and prepared them to challenge the foreigners who dominated their countries. They did this even when the colonial officials made it clear that they intended to stay on as long as they could. These officials regularly demonstrated that local anti-colonial resistance did not have a chance until the two world wars exposed the soft underbelly of European modernity.

What captured the local imagination between the wars was the idea of popular sovereignty. In India and China, the elites saw how this had promoted nationalism and socialism in Europe and the Americas. Many were attracted to social activism and political participation and were inspired by how freedom would enable them to limit hereditary privilege and ultimately replace traditional forms of authority. They therefore demanded political rights and began to develop the institutions that could bring social justice to the disadvantaged. They learnt that if their demands were resisted or poorly handled, that could lead to popular protests and even revolutionary movements.

Those leaders who focused on the capitalism behind the empires looked to the working class in England and studied how they were successfully politicised in various parts of Europe. That development reached its climax in the 1917 Russian Revolution that overturned the Tsarist Empire. The Bolshevik victory had little direct impact on imperial rule outside Europe. But its open and consistent opposition to imperialism resonated with colonial subjects. In our region, it helped to arouse national consciousness in the Philippines, Indonesia, Burma and Vietnam.

During that period of rapid change, Southeast Asia began to see the differences between the many components of Enlightenment civilisation that the national empires claimed to be modern. The new nations also observed how other civilisations were responding by choosing to modernise each in its own way. This helped our region's leaders to think afresh about how they too could develop their modern national cultures.

In the world of new national consciousness, the colony of Singapore stood out as a city whose people of various origins used the city as a centre for their activities between land and sea before deciding to make it their base or home. The authorities who were determined to make the free port a success encouraged the acts of *merantau* that swelled a population with the characteristics of a plural society.

Having long lost its place as a political centre, Singapore did not have a distinctive local culture. From a barely populated part of the Johor Empire, it started afresh to become part of the Straits Settlements governed from India. Even after it became a separate colony, it was primarily a link in the British imperial chain that was used as a business hub mainly by peripatetic Malays, Chinese and Indians. Most of them brought their cultures with them, cultures inspired by the Indic of India, the Islamic in Nusantara and the Indian Ocean and the Sinic of China's southern provinces.

When European imperialism reached its heyday just before World War I, British Malaya was conceived with its centre in Singapore. That Malaya was what the island city would become part of when the war ended in 1945. As with the rest of Southeast Asia, this Malaya conformed to the regional norm of having an imperial administration and distinct local cultures shaped by the living civilisations that were brought there by its various communities.

The civilisation of the European Enlightenment after World War II was facing conditions that needed to be modernised anew. As their national empires were dismantled, they observed how the three ancient civilisations were each modernising selectively. They were also confronted by the people they had ruled over, whose newly independent nation-states had been opposed to imperialism. Altogether, there was a new awareness that the Enlightenment was only one phase of the modern. Those in Southeast Asia inspired by new ideas of modernity were confident that their own past experiences of learning from neighbouring civilisations made their local cultures strong. That would enable them to learn afresh about the modern they really needed. If they succeeded, the national cultures and identities that emerged would demonstrate how modern nation-states might live with different civilisations. That could then give our region a useful and distinct role in a new world system.

Question-and-Answer Session
Moderated by Professor Elaine Ho

Prof Elaine Ho: Thank you, Prof Wang, for a very insightful lecture, and for helping us to better understand how global forces have converged geographically in the region, as well as how cultures in our region responded, adapted, proved resilient and even challenged these global forces they came into contact with. On this note, there are probably many thoughts running through the minds of our audience members and I would like to invite you to ask questions.

Participant: I have a question about your thoughts on the Padri movement. What I know is that it was a civil war against the Minangkabau society. What do you think of the Padri movement, since you mentioned it in your lecture?

Prof Wang Gungwu: I was very brief about the Padri movement, but it represented a very strong effort to bring more Islamic learning to Southeast Asia. Among the Minangkabau at that time, *adat* was primary. That was the primary basis on which the society was structured and *adat* had traditions that to the purists in Islam were considered not to be appropriate for Islam, and they tried to persuade the Minangkabau to abandon these *adat* features, which they had practised for a long time. And it was that conflict that led to some of the Minangkabau turning to the Dutch for help against the more violent members of the Padri movement who started a war against the Minangkabau.

But that's the brief story. I don't think I can go into the details of that. It was a considerable war that spanned a long time. It took quite a long time before the Minangkabau turned more Islamic themselves.

Participant: I was most fascinated by your discussion about the Indic religious civilisation, especially in the area of Buddhism. You mentioned how Buddhism was subsequently rejected by India and how it declined as a major religion in South Asia, but in recent years, we see how India has been using Buddhism as part of diplomacy. We have seen the revival of the Nalanda Project and also how India's Prime Minister, Narendra Modi, has used Buddhism as soft power diplomacy. I wonder how we can make sense of modern nation-states using religion as part of their soft power diplomacy. This is also in tandem with using history to justify a country's foreign policy objective.

Prof Wang: I will touch on the developments in India's last 10 to 20 years in my next lecture. In general, the question is a good one. The revival of a broader Hindu or Indic perspective on the world has been going on for some time. But the question of the Buddhism that was developed elsewhere outside of India, and which does not fit into the picture that the Hindus themselves see of Buddhism — that remains a problem. This is because the examples that I gave were about what happened to Buddhism in Burma, Thailand and Cambodia. They are not part of that story that Narendra Modi is speaking about in India. That's not how he would see Buddhism. Buddhism has also become localised and nationalised elsewhere outside of India. That's the point which was really interesting to me.

In that Indic worldview, it was possible for the Buddhist aspect of it to totally change elsewhere and yet remain linked with its Indic roots. Till this day, I would say that Buddhism in the whole of East Asia and Southeast Asia will still refer to India as the homeland of where the ideas came from, and speak with great respect for India as the homeland of Buddhism. But Buddhist practices in those countries are not attractive to the people of India because they have been locally transformed into something quite distinct. So that fascinates me. The Indic worldview can be seen as tremendously elastic, and it can be taken out of India and developed elsewhere in different ways. Yet, at the same time, those Buddhists still look to India as their home, but the Indians don't quite recognise the Indic roots that are found in Buddhism practised elsewhere.

Participant: In your last lecture, you spoke about the arrival of Raffles in Singapore in 1819 and the modernity that was brought in at that time. Singapore started with a very small cohort of administrators who were benign and non-interventionist, which is very similar to Hong Kong.

However, when you talk about Singapore, we have a government which I believe has been very benignly interventionist. They brought us from third world to first. While Hong Kong was looking out more to the Western world as "one country, two systems", it is now looking like "one country, one system", with very centralised features. What are your comments?

Prof Wang: I've written elsewhere comparing Singapore and Hong Kong. I won't go into the details of that but I would say that from the very beginning, the two situations were fundamentally different. In the case of Singapore, it was more a question of Anglo-Dutch relations in a Nusantara Islamic world and a small base for commercial strategic use. Whereas for Hong Kong, when the British took it from China, it was from the very beginning a special problem because they were taking Hong Kong from a territory that was a very huge empire.

At the time, the Qing Government didn't feel sorry about losing Hong Kong. They had hardly noticed Hong Kong themselves, so they were not concerned that the British wanted it, and they ceded it in the Treaty of Nanking. They were more concerned with defending the Yangtze River, and not letting the British get further north. To Qing China, losing Hong Kong wasn't much of a problem. From the beginning, the whole situation was different because if you look at the development in Hong Kong almost from day one, it was always a sort of "one country, two systems". The one country was always China, because almost the whole Hong Kong population came down from China. In fact, at least 95 per cent of Hong Kong's population today is from China. So, it never changed.

It was one country insofar as all the population were Chinese, but it was two systems. In other words, the Chinese were living in Hong Kong under the British in some aspects, but they were also under the Chinese in other aspects. Hong Kong was in and out of China all the time — there were hardly any checks and balances or borders to speak of, and people from Guangdong and Fujian were in and out of Hong Kong for the next hundred years without feeling any particular difference when they moved between China and Hong Kong.

The British also did not see the Hong Kong people as different from those from China. The British were not concerned as long as Hong Kong people followed British law, accepted the fact that the British had privileges in the city's trading and operations, and that it was a base for the British to do other things in China. The Qing Government also didn't care, and even after the republic was established under Sun Yat-sen, the republic didn't have time to care too much about Hong Kong, and left the city alone because it was convenient. In the minds of the Chinese people, Hong Kong was always China. However, Hong Kong was legally under the British, which is why I have suggested that Hong Kong had been functioning as one country, two systems from the very beginning. It never really was a British colony per se. It was a British colony by name, as well as in law and administration, but in terms of socio-cultural affairs and the way the economy functioned, it was so much part of China that it was impossible to separate Hong Kong from China in real life.

So, from that point of view, that was totally different from Singapore. And when you mentioned the British Government's non-interventionist governance in Hong Kong, I think they were actually non-interventionists in Singapore as well. This was particularly because they were very sensitive about the fact that Singapore was in the Islamic world. The British were fully aware of the Christian experience with Muslims in the past, which went back to the Crusades. There was a general understanding and sensitivity about dealing with the Islamic world, whereas the British found that the Chinese were very different.

The Chinese had no worries about Christianity or God. They were much more practical people that the British could do business with, so there was no need to intervene in Hong Kong. The sensitivities were minimal, and it is quite interesting when you contrast Hong Kong and Singapore in this manner. From the very beginning, the British military did not touch Chinese society in Hong Kong. They basically left it to develop on its own, whereas in Singapore, they made an effort. But this did not make them successful. In the end, there were just too few British officials, and too many *merantau* people who came from all over the region. As such, it was hard for the British to intervene in Singapore.

But in general, they were much more aware of the differences between Hong Kong and Singapore. I was struck by this because I spent 10 years in Hong Kong, and looked at some of the laws and practices that were introduced in Hong Kong, which were deliberately different from those of Singapore. I used to ask Hong Kong people why that was the case, and they made the point that Singapore was alien to the imperial system. On the other hand, Hong Kong was part and parcel of a bigger commercial world. It was not so much an imperial mission in Hong Kong as a commercial mission. In comparison, Singapore became a strategic base for the whole imperial empire particularly between Britain and the Pacific, including Australia and New Zealand. It was strategically absolutely essential to keep Singapore, so for the British not to intervene in Singapore at all would have been unthinkable. But they were also very careful. I'm very struck by the extent to which they were very sensitive to the feelings of the ordinary people even while they were intervening.

Participant: You highlighted a distinction between local culture and civilisation in the process of nation and empire building. I tried to connect this with your previous point about the Chinese civilisation. For policymakers, it is probably difficult to change civilisations. They can try to change culture using cultural policies, but not civilisations. So civilisation seems to me a given. It's less likely to be changed by policymakers. Does this mean that civilisations, and Chinese civilisation in particular, are more likely to persist for a long time as compared to cultures?

Prof Wang: This is a big question. I would have to try and simplify it as much as I can. The Chinese always had a recognised hierarchy of values. And I would define a civilisation as one where its ideas, such as that of morality, benevolence and even compassion, are desired and recognised as universal. They have a borderless appeal. And the Chinese did have a sense that their classical learning and values of Confucius (as well as other great thinkers) were borderless. Anybody can learn from them because it would be beneficial for them. They had no borders.

But the Chinese themselves also recognised local cultures, which were, in Mandarin, *fengsu xiguan* (风俗习惯), the local ways of doing things. They do not necessarily have anything to do with the classical wisdom that the great Chinese philosophers thought of. These local cultures are perfectly Chinese as well, but because they are local, they're practised by the ordinary people, although the locals recognised that there was something above them which was universal. This understanding is extremely old.

For example, some of this distinction could be seen after the Song dynasty, when the Chinese classics were printed, and people could buy and read them. Since everyone could read the classics, and they became quite common, the local cultures became more intimate with them. Local cultures became more recognised and closer to the greater Sinic civilisation. And in the last few hundred years, there were efforts to say that "Chinese-ness" could be broadened to include these local cultures, the *fengsu xiguan*. Those were also part of Chinese civilisation.

As I've previously said, local cultures don't transmit their ideologies and do not attract other people outside those cultures. It is the voice of classical texts that appeals to the masses. The local cultures are very local, and it is hard for those outside the cultures to be attracted to them. For example, in places like Guangzhou, Fujian or even different parts of northern China, the local culture is so peculiar to these areas that Chinese people outside these parts of China don't completely identify with these cultures.

For the ancient part of this view, I won't try to explain it because there are too many features for this. In modern terms, words like "civilisation" and "culture" have their own translations in Chinese because there was no precise Chinese word for "civilisation" or "culture" as understood in the West. Once those ideologies were adopted, it then became clear that *wenming* (文明) is more universal and can be claimed to be borderless, whereas *wenhua* (文化) is something peculiar to the locality or the country in question. In Chinese today, there's a difference between *zhonghua wenming* (中华文明) and *zhongguo wenhua* (中国文化), and again I'm trying to simplify in order to explain these terms. For example, *zhongguo wenhua* is a term that was unrecognisable to the Chinese in the past. This is because there was no such thing as *zhongguo wenhua*; it was all either *wenming* of the larger Sinic civilisation or local cultures.

But *zhongguo wenhua* exists now because China is now recognised as a nation-state. Whether they can define it quite clearly to themselves and to the rest of the world is still an issue. People say that China is a civilisation state, that it's a multinational, multiethnic state, and different words have been used to explain what China is like. There is a distinction between this nationalistic culture and *zhonghua wenming*, which has to do with the Sinic civilisation that has been continuous for so long, and has been transmitted to people in Vietnam, Korea and Japan, and other people who have adopted it over time. This also applies to the Chinese who are outside China, for example in Southeast Asia or elsewhere in the world, who would identify with *zhonghua wenming*. However, it is not so clear if this group identifies with *zhongguo wenhua*.

I'm using these terms now, and I'll speak a little bit more about this in my last lecture. As for the Chinese adoption of the words *wenming* and *wenhua*, once you try to distinguish between them, you will see that *zhonghua wenming* can claim to be universal and borderless, and *zhongguo wenhua* cannot be, because it belongs to China, to *zhongguo*. This refers to national culture. This is why we must first distinguish between the two, before it's possible to talk about any other things to do with the relationship with China.

Prof Ho: For those of you who are interested in Prof Wang's first lecture, he differentiated between the ideas of culture and civilisation. Actually Prof Wang, your response leads very nicely to this next question from Facebook. I might just rephrase the question a little. In what sense can a civilisation be said to be inferior, particularly in the context of what you shared in terms of European powers trying to "civilise" our region? Is it necessarily the case that certain civilisations are more inferior than others? And more specifically, was Sinic civilisation inferior to the Western civilisations?

Prof Wang: Well, I think this takes me to the subject today, which is about the Enlightened Modern. These national empires that embraced the Enlightenment Modernity embodied the wealth and capitalistic power that enabled them to become so dominant in the world, so the criteria that measures the degree of superiority of a civilisation are actually very material. It is material progress that is used to measure success and civilisation, with markers such as scientific discovery, the quality of technology and outdoing rivals in economic affairs. These national empires came to Asia where there have been civilisations long before the Enlightenment period. And yet very clearly, from the time they came here, they would deem the civilisations in our region as ancient and no longer meaningful.

The debate between modern and ancient itself is a very interesting one. It was opened up in the late 18th century in Europe, and the debate went on for quite a while. It was among classical scholars to begin with, but essentially what they wanted to distinguish was that there was an ancient world. In fact, in European terms, they already recognised the ancient world, the classical world, which they admired, but which they also recognised as the past. To them, this classical, ancient world did wonderful things before, but was no longer relevant to them because it had been superseded by modern ideologies and benchmarks. For example, church authority is seen as backward and was opposed because it was deemed unhelpful to the opening of the mind. In this sense, science was actually used against church authority. Some examples of the modern mind taking over from traditional ways of thinking include prioritising the rights of the citizens over rulers. And so the Europeans used this same set of criteria to benchmark other societies and civilisations.

They looked at all the other civilisations and considered them ancient in spite of how great they might have been in the past. To them, Indian classics may be wonderful, but as far as the West was concerned, the Indian people were backward because they could not free themselves from these practices and traditions, which were no longer helpful in the modern world that they deemed more important. All this was part of the Enlightenment. It did not mean to attack others to begin with, since it actually stemmed from within the Christian European civilisation itself. Western critics were trying to show that there was something wrong with ancient practices. They were convinced that they had to go beyond the ancient to become modern, and by being modern you could guarantee yourself progress. In order to advance, the Enlightenment believed that a civilisation needed critical thinking and reason as well as scientific methodologies. Capitalism was one of the instruments of achieving that in economic terms, and building empires was the other way. Empires and this modern Western civilisation could bring civilisation to the rest of the world because they believed that they were superior.

Prof Ho: Let me pose this last question for Prof Wang. In the previous lecture, Prof Wang said that Chinese culture would be poorer without the absorption of Buddhism from India. Does Prof Wang see China learning from India again, and thereby be tremendously enriched once more? This is a somewhat provocative question.

Prof Wang: There was a time where the Chinese people were very open to learning from the outside world. I think modern historians agree, more or less, that somewhere from the Tang dynasty onwards, the Chinese people were very open and that is when Buddhism and other forms of foreign ideas, techniques and technologies were adopted and absorbed into China.

In fact, between the fall of the Han dynasty down to the Tang dynasty, China was very open, and Buddhism is the best example of this openness because it was so powerful as a religion. It completely took over China, and even today, every Chinese person more or less has a Buddhist background as a result of that.

After the Song dynasty, the Chinese tried to bring all their knowledge together to become the core of a new Chinese understanding of the world. We now call this Neo-Confucianism, and those Confucian texts were reinterpreted, drawing upon Buddhist sutras, Taoist literature and so on. All this was done to try to encompass all of the knowledge into a more perfect understanding of the world. After that, the Chinese became less open. In fact, everyone noticed that Chinese philosophical thinking reached its peak in the Song dynasty. And then after the Mongol conquest, and the Ming revival (the Ming actually became very traditionalist), the Chinese adopted Song Neo-Confucianism and made that the basis of their own examination system. That ideology dominated the examination system for the next 500 to 600 years.

From then on, the Chinese became more closed off to external ideas. For example, when the Jesuits arrived in China with other new ideas, they reported that on the whole, the Chinese were not receptive to these ideas. This was the case even though a few Chinese realised that some of these new ideas were worth thinking about, particularly some of their new observations in geography, mathematics and astronomy. These were practised in Europe and brought by the Jesuits to China. Some Chinese did recognise these novel ideas as important, but in general the mandarins decided that they had already found their core ideologies, and were resistant to bringing in new ideas. So when the young generation went against Chinese civilisation at the end of the 19th century, they recognised the Chinese civilisation's retreat from openness. The younger generation wanted to overthrow this system and replace it with a new one, one that demonstrated a willingness to learn. And I think this is exactly what they had done.

The question is: What did the Chinese choose to learn from the West? During the crucial period between the 1930s and 1950s, I think big decisions were made. In fact, by 1949, to everyone's surprise, the Chinese Communist Party won. That was a major shift in what they learnt. They were learning from the West. They wanted to be modern. They wanted to be a new, powerful nation-state like the West. In fact, some of the Chinese went as far as to say that they should learn everything from the West. And today, it may be possible to say that up to at least 80 per cent of what is happening in China is actually inspired by the West.

However, there remains a reserved area in which the Chinese have retained their own practices and beliefs without borrowing from the West. And this is what the battle is about today. They learnt so well from the West in some things, but were not willing to learn about other things. I believe that made the West feel threatened. Because now the Chinese have the capacity having learnt what they deemed useful from the West, but also they have not accepted some of what the West has considered to be paramount ideas that should be valued. This is where I think the battle is. I'm oversimplifying, but that's essentially what I'm trying to say.

Prof Ho: Thank you very much, Prof Wang, for all the insightful ideas and thoughts that you've shared with us.

Lecture IV
LIVING CIVILISATIONS AND NATIONAL CULTURES

LECTURE IV

In my first lecture, I stressed that our region did not even have its own name until after World War II. We have now come to the end of that war, so it is time to get back to the moment when the region began to see itself as having a common past and about to have a common future. When I accepted the S R Nathan Fellowship, I said that I would focus on the region called Southeast Asia. It was centred on Singapore as its *ujong tanah*, a place populated largely with *merantau* people whose wanderings made the port city a plural society before it was forced to become a nation-state.

Southeast Asia was conceived by British Empire builders as a strategic concept to rescue as much of their imperial interests as possible after two disastrous wars. The Australians and New Zealanders were distant beneficiaries. The Americans were agreeable because that supplemented their maritime projections in the Western Pacific. The French, Dutch and Portuguese were grateful to have support to return to the region. And during the next five decades, the region was the biggest gainer. Its new nation-states discovered that they not only shared a common past and had similar post-war interests but could also build a common future together. It was to understand Southeast Asia and the place of Singapore in the region where I have chosen to examine the difference between cultures and civilisations.

A Divided Enlightenment World

The catalyst for a new world order was the war fought by an Asian power — imperial Japan. The Japanese claimed to have liberated our region from Western colonialism and that helped to reveal the fatal weakness in that Enlightenment civilisation. They also tried to prepare the Philippines, Indonesia and Burma for possible nationhood. In each of those colonies, there were leaders who welcomed that help, but many others were sceptical and hoped that the Japanese would be defeated. At the same time, Japan demonstrated how their response to Enlightenment modernity had helped to strengthen Japanese national culture. This had encouraged local nationalist leaders to resist the colonial powers that tried to return and they made every effort to throw them out.

As the weakest of those powers, the Dutch found that they could not subdue the nationalists who embarked on a revolutionary war and insisted on keeping all of the Netherlands East Indies as the Republic of Indonesia. The French faced three potential rival nations in their "Indochina" and hoped that they could stay on longer. When the Cold War came to the region after Nationalist China fell to the Chinese Communist Party (CCP), the United States (US) encouraged the French to resist Vietnamese demands for an independent nation-state. As for the British, they were realistic enough to see that they would have to leave India and decided to let Burma go free. By concentrating on Malaya, Singapore and a few scattered ports and islands, they hoped to stay as long as they could.

In short, there were multiple changes to the national borders drawn up in our region by the European empires. Probably the most important were those that were identified by British strategists as separating Southeast Asia from China and India. That way, Southeast Asia could provide a separate theatre for future political and military operations. This reflected the wider rethinking that sought to find a new geopolitical framework that would enable powerful countries to settle their conflicting interests and help to bring peace to the world.

During World War II, the eventual victors led by the US, Soviet Union and Britain agreed that the aggressive national empires had undermined the Enlightenment Project that represented modern civilisation. However, they thought that the project was essentially progressive and could be reformed and revived. That would require making major corrections to the civilising mission to stop powerful nation-states from fighting one another again. The chastened powers thus tried to reinvent themselves. The British and the French succeeded in keeping their spheres of influence by tying former colonies to a nominal commonwealth of nations. Both still had the resources to help their former colonies get started as nation-states. But they were aware that the modern world would no longer tolerate national empires and that other civilisations were modernising so that they could stand up against the idea that the Western Modern would always be dominant.

The West led by the US and the Soviet Union emerged as the real victors of World War II. They saved Europe from Nazi Germany and East Asia from Imperial Japan and still saw themselves as the leaders of modern civilisation. Both were products of the Christian European civilisation that produced the Age of Enlightenment, but they could not agree as to what parts of that Enlightenment should serve as the core of the renewed civilisation. Nor could they agree on the means to be employed to achieve the results they wanted.

The liberal Americans focused on the idea that freedom was a universal value. It was the key to the capitalism and economic development that made the West so prosperous and powerful. They gave priority to the democratic rights of the individual. The Soviet Union in the hands of the Stalinists rejected the power of capitalists to enrich themselves at the expense of their workers. It concentrated on a Marx–Leninist idea that only a strong party-state using central planning methods could decide how wealth should be redistributed.

The two superpowers knew that they would become rivals in world affairs and acted to divide Europe into zones of contestation. They also set out to convert the rest of the world to their respective interpretations of what was progressive. They were especially sensitive to the aspirations of the former colonies of the Western Europeans that were now embarked on nation building.

In one vital area, the US led the way. They examined the lessons of the failed League of Nations that it did not join, even though it was US President Woodrow Wilson who worked hard to set it up after World War I. President Roosevelt made sure this time round that the US would play the key role to design the United Nations (UN) to replace that League. This UN would avoid the earlier mistake of having empires like Britain, France, Japan and Italy as permanent members of an executive council. Instead, the UN Security Council's five permanent members would be given veto powers against decisions that any one of them disagreed with.

However, the most important advance was to agree that every UN member, however large or small, was a nation-state of equal status. There would no longer be empires. All the former territories of an empire could only join as nation-states, and as each was decolonised, the new states created would be admitted as full-fledged members. This was a huge step forward. With that foundation, the UN set out to establish a comprehensive set of principles to enable their institutions to develop a peaceful world order.

The Enlightenment spirit here reflected the borderless civilisation that had been dominant in the fields of science and technology and in areas of economic development. With feelings of admiration and hope, I recall the debates about what kind of Malaya our future nation would be like. My generation saw the UN as the guarantor of national sovereignty, and an institution that would enable the world to avoid future wars. It was proof that the Enlightenment Modern could be rescued and redefined so that all civilisations would seek progress together. The new nation-states could now concentrate on building national cultures that would frame their future identities with lofty principles.

Figure 1. United Nations Office in Geneva

Source: Photo taken by Xabi Oregi.

It soon became clear that saving key parts of Enlightenment civilisation would not be enough. Almost immediately after the UN was launched, local wars had to be fought against the return to any kind of imperialism by the more powerful states. In Europe, the US and the Soviet Union found themselves confronting each other in the Cold War. Although both sides avoided the language of empires, imperial overtones reappeared as they each geared up to gather dependent or client states. Their rivalry was reframed in ideological terms that were drawn from earlier phases of the Enlightenment. Some of the rhetoric was couched in terms of good versus evil as each side called for all nation-states to choose between the American-led West and the Soviet bloc in Eurasia.

In Asia, the most dramatic change came with the victory of the CCP. The UN framework was tested when the People's Republic of China (PRC) sided with the Soviet Union and was denied entry into the UN as China. Thereafter, the Security Council was used as a battleground where the US, the Republic of China (ROC) and the remaining two empires (Britain and France) opposed the Soviet Union. This stopped the PRC from taking its place in the UN for over 20 years. The decision demonstrated that a gathering of nation-states could not be an instrument for global civilisation if the national interests of superpowers always prevailed. In other words, the UN too had a fatal weakness.

For the next decades, it was clear that the imperial past had not gone away. The US and the Soviet Union were virtual empires, each with "security partners" that fought through their proxies. In our region, that was done via a hot war in Vietnam. This was a dangerous threat to the new nation-states which had communist movements that challenged the nationalist leadership.

For the two superpowers, the next 40 years became a tug-of-war with every state asked to join one side or the other. Fortunately, their direct confrontation in the Cuban Missile Crisis of 1962 was the only time when the whole world felt the threat of a third world war. Learning from that experience, the superpowers fought by other means under the MAD shadow of "mutually assured destruction".[1] It was a struggle where the US had a clear advantage. Through its global maritime power, its free market economy was far superior to the largely continental economy that the Soviet Union depended on. Outside of Eurasia, the Soviet Union struggled to keep up, and even lost the support of Mao Zedong. After that, with China's success following Deng Xiaoping's economic reforms, the competition for global development moved to Asia.

Thus, the US defended Western Europe successfully and the Soviet Union system rapidly collapsed. With victory for one side of the Enlightenment civilisation, the US became the world's sole super nation-state. As victor of the ideological war, it saw itself as the beacon for universal values. Its all-round power would now enable it to act as the guardian of global civilisation. In that role, American leaders set out to demonstrate that they were ready to behave like a civilisation-state.

---

[1] Mutually assured destruction (MAD) is a principle of deterrence that posits a nuclear attack by one superpower would be met with a nuclear counterattack such that both the attacker and the defender would be annihilated.

Figure 2. Map of the Soviet Union (1989)

Source: Courtesy of the University of Texas Libraries, The University of Texas at Austin. Retrieved from: https://maps.lib.utexas.edu/maps/commonwealth/soviet_union_admin_1989.jpg.

Southeast Asia clearly benefitted from the peace that ensued. The region's self-discovery four decades earlier had enabled it to appreciate how its respective local cultures had grown in confidence by learning from its neighbouring civilisations. They continued to do that even when they were under Western rule. Despite being under Cold War shadows, they seized every opportunity to build their nation-states to meet their needs. Not least, they observed how the civilisations from which they had learnt in the past were modernising to deal with every new challenge posed.

All four ancient civilisations — the Indic, the Sinic, the Islamic and the Christian European — were living civilisations. The Christian European civilisation had borne the brunt of the initial changes in Europe itself, as the Enlightenment had developed by challenging the civilisation's spiritual authority. But it continued to stand for spiritual values that had wider appeal while its missionaries followed the national empires around the world. In Southeast Asia, it remained strong in the Philippines and won local converts in most countries even after they gained independence. In some, Christian European civilisation was also seen as protectors of native minorities.

The peoples from the three other civilisations — the Indic, the Islamic and the Sinic — continued to interact within our region's cultures. They saw how the new nation-states had internalised what they wanted from their imperial masters. Although some had their respect for tradition weakened, to the extent of admitting that parts of their heritage were backward, they were all prepared to renew their civilisations so that they could compete and prosper.

One thing was clear. The living civilisations acknowledged the vitality and dynamism of the Enlightenment Modern. They recognised that this civilisation was borderless and, at its best, stood for reason, the advantages of freedom and for the equal rights of their citizens. They sought material progress through education and professional training and took advantage of the revised Enlightenment modernity that made everything available for them to learn. Some of their elites went further to reject the claims of transcendental faiths in favour of secular governance but allowed practices that met people's spiritual needs.

Southeast Asia: A Modern Region

The full story is a complex one and this is not the place to tell it. Let me return to Southeast Asia to outline the way its peoples sought to develop their national cultures. I shall not cover each country in turn. Instead, the focus will be on two developments from which each state had much to learn. The developments encapsulated the process of re-education that also helped to shape the region's understanding of its common interests.

The first was what our leaders experienced at the Bandung Conference of 1955. The other was what they managed to learn when they turned a half-ASEAN (Association of Southeast Asian Nations) into the full

Figure 3. Closing Plenary Meeting of the Bandung Conference (1955)

Note: The photo depicts the scene of the closing plenary meeting of the Asian-African Conference in Bandung. The head of the Indian delegation, Prime Minister Jawaharlal Nehru, was giving his remarks. It was taken on 24 April 1955.
Source: Daftar Arsip Foto Kementerian Penerangan (Kempen) Wilayah Jawa Barat No. JB 5501–558.

10-member organisation it now is. Both were examples of what our national leaders saw in the living civilisations with which they were in contact. Each new nation adapted readily to whatever served its needs. At the same time, each discovered distinct ways of dealing with their common interests. They seemed able to do this with a confidence that came from centuries of dealing with living civilisations.

Most historians would agree that the Bandung Conference promised more than it could deliver. Some would argue that it was mostly sound and fury that showed that even when all the civilisations got together, they had nothing better to offer. Its declared purpose was to bring together those members of the UN who were opposed to the world being divided between two antagonistic blocs represented by the Warsaw Pact states and those in the North Atlantic Treaty Organisation (NATO). In other words, the

Figure 4. Map of the Warsaw Pact States (Red) and the NATO States (Blue)

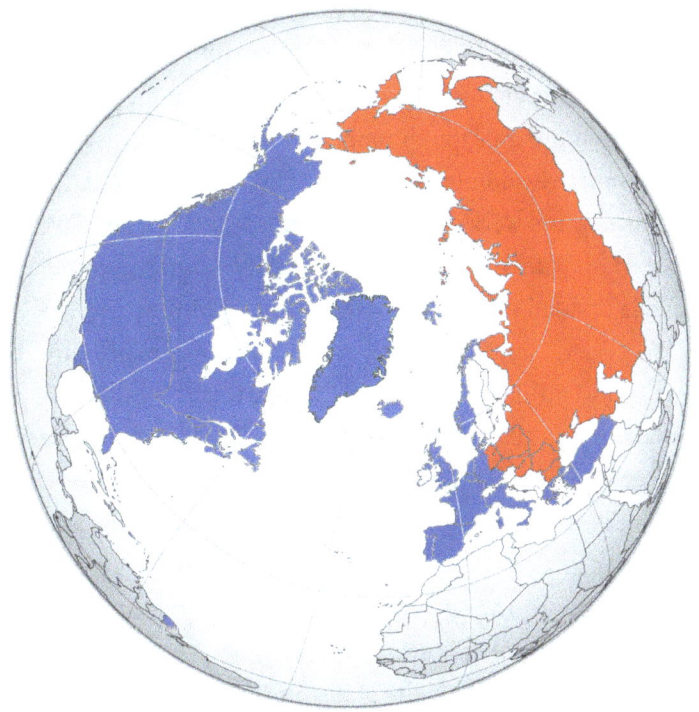

Source: "NATO vs. Warsaw (1949–1990)" by Heitor Carvalho Jorge. This image is licensed under CC BY-SA 3.0.

conference wanted to free itself from the divided Enlightenment Modern with which each side set out to destroy the other.

Of the 29 nations that attended, eight represented Southeast Asia: North and South Vietnam, as well as six others that were already independent — namely Thailand, the Philippines, Laos, Indonesia, Burma and Cambodia. The Colony of Singapore, the Protectorates of Malaya and Brunei, their British masters, together with other permanent members of the UN, were not invited. Representatives of various civilisations were present: the Indic by India and the Buddhist states, the Islamic by several states of the Middle East and the Sinic by the PRC and Japan. The conference was hosted in our region by its largest nation, Indonesia, a country that had found inspiration from three civilisations, and was led by nationalist leaders who also identified with the Enlightenment Modern. The participants could be described as those who were reacting to a flawed world order. But it could also be seen as an effort to demonstrate the combined power of modernised civilisations that did not want to be dominated by the Enlightenment West. It could even claim that its slogans were attractive to half the world's population. It was even followed up with an Afro-Asian Solidarity Conference and a Summit in Yugoslavia that led to the larger Non-Aligned Movement.

The so-called Bandung spirit remained as an expression of good intentions and wishful thinking. But it did show that — although proud of their civilisations — all the new nations aspired to become modern. It also showed that it was unable to influence the course of the Cold War. Nevertheless, it provided an indication that Southeast Asia could become an active player in global affairs even when conditions were so difficult.

This takes me to the second example of our region's potential, the formation of ASEAN. This is a remarkable story. I had referred earlier to the exceptional fact that half the states in our region were maritime in outlook while the other half was continental in orientation. What was also significant was that the Cold War was from beginning to end one between the maritime powers led by the US and the continental bloc led by the Soviet Union. Also, the new states of Southeast Asia could not fail to notice that the American allies, imperial Britain and France, were returning to the region. When these three became members of what was called the Southeast Asia Treaty Organisation (SEATO) that was established as a local version of NATO with only the Philippines and Thailand joining, it reduced SEATO's credibility as a regional organisation. It was a sign that our region would prefer to develop its own identity and not be locked onto a cold war that could be inimical to the interests of the independent nation-states.

But there was no alternative to this SEATO that united all the anti-communist states of the region to prevent the Soviet Union and the PRC from advancing south via Vietnam. Only Indonesia under President Sukarno and his nationalist colleagues, still basking in the Bandung spirit, stood firm against an organisation that was inspired by what they saw as former colonial powers. When the Federation of Malaya became independent, its Prime Minister Tunku Abdul Rahman also chose to stay out of SEATO. But Sukarno opposed the formation of a Greater Malaysia that included northern Borneo and launched his Konfrontasi campaign. By this time, it was clear that Indonesia's Parti Kommunis (PKI) was very close to the CCP in China. An abortive Gestapu coup brought the struggle to the open and led to the destruction of all left-wing forces in the country. The new President Suharto then agreed to a local regional organisation and ASEAN was formed. This was related to the British withdrawal from northern Borneo to allow its formation as a major state in the heart of the region, the Malaysia Federation. While it also marked the alternative that Bandung had stood for, ASEAN also represented the region's desire to stamp a local identity on the decolonisation process. Such a shared effort to protect collective interests could be said to have marked a turning point in regional self-awareness.

ASEAN had a modest beginning in the midst of the Vietnam War. Its founding five members included the newly independent Republic of Singapore. Those who saw it as nothing more than a political club on the side of the US and its allies expected little from the establishment. Indeed, it could do little to affect the course of the hot war nearby that the US was losing. Each could therefore concentrate on nation building and reshaping their complex societies. Indonesia, in particular, had recently faced deep divisions among its widespread communities and its economy needed a great deal of foreign assistance and investment. Both Malaysia and Singapore were undergoing a painful process of virtual decoupling. Malaysia was in a much happier position, having almost doubled its territory and rid itself of a dissatisfied Singapore. As for the new city-state Singapore, it had the challenging task to build its plural society into a secure and prosperous nation-state.

Figure 5. Founding Members of ASEAN in Bangkok, Thailand (1967)

From left: Foreign ministers Thanat Khoman of Thailand, Narciso R. Ramos of the Philippines, S. Rajaratnam of Singapore, Abdul Razak of Malaysia and Adam Malik of Indonesia.
Source: Ministry of Information and the Arts Collection, courtesy of National Archives of Singapore.

All five ASEAN countries had one other thing in common. Each was committed to becoming modern in as many ways as possible while defending the country's mix of local cultures. At the core of modernity were capital investment and the re-education of a new generation of skilled personnel who could provide the technological advancement that each country urgently needed. The nationalist leaders were very aware that they also had powerful protectors in the US and its allies against those who sought to overturn the established order in the name of people's revolution.

Fortunately for the ASEAN states, before the US lost the Vietnam War, President Nixon had succeeded in wooing Mao Zedong's China away from the Soviet Union. By doing so, it enabled the new partners to stop the expansion of Vietnamese power into Cambodia and Laos. The role that the five ASEAN states, now joined by the Brunei Sultanate, played in helping Cambodia preserve its sovereignty is well known. But it is important to stress ASEAN's input in that success. That was a major step in showing its members that the Association could exercise agency within the region. The experience encouraged the region's leaders to pursue the goal of uniting with communist states in the region to extend ASEAN membership to all the Southeast Asian states. It was a huge test of diplomatic skill, discovery of common interests and rare patience. Not least was the commitment to modernity combined with sensitivity to local cultural differences that each member had cultivated.

Singapore was in an exceptional position, bearing in mind that the republic was a totally new creation with a history only two years older than ASEAN itself. From a modern port city to a brief period as the 14th state

Figure 6. US Soldiers During the Vietnam War (1967)

Source: "Vietnam War 1967 — US Marines" by manhhai. This image is licensed under CC BY 2.0.

of a new federation that was culturally linked to the Nusantara world, the republic seemed unprepared to be a player in a new regional organisation. However, its leaders had long shared their lives with the descendants of *merantau* peoples from different cultures and civilisations. In addition, they had actively reached out beyond the region in order to better understand the special needs of a modern plural society.

The Threat of National Cultures

By 1999, all 10 states in Southeast Asia had joined ASEAN and it was now in a position to represent the whole region. That became possible in part because the Cold War had ended and a new world order had emerged. There were different geopolitical calculations to be made in the context of the new Enlightenment civilisation led by the US. Those who believed that the US was the only light on the hill expected a new stage of globalisation under its leadership. Those who believed that there were other modern civilisations foresaw that there would come a time when powerful nation-states would clash in the name of their civilisations. Indeed, there took place a largely academic debate between Francis Fukuyama and Samuel Huntington as to whether that could happen. The matter came to be tested when the US acted swiftly to respond to the jihadist attacks on the New York twin towers in September 2001. It was surprising when the US, as the world's most powerful nation-state, confidently invaded two sovereign states Iraq and Afghanistan. With only the support of its Cold War allies, there were echoes of the national empire acting in the name of civilisation against barbarism.

The US clearly had the military power to do whatever it wanted. It had the measure of the civilisations that had been modernising. It could see that there was the lack of a superstate among the Islamic faithful in the Middle East and North Africa. The divisions in Turkic and Iranian Central Asia as well as on the Indian subcontinent were also likely to remain permanent. As for the syncretic nature of Nusantara Islam, that had been shaped to serve local cultures and was not designed for global conflicts.

Figure 7. Mohammad Reza Pahlavi, the Last Shah of Iran (1970)

Note: Mohammad Reza Pahlavi was overthrown in the Iranian Revolution of 1979.
Source: "Shahi Mohammad Reza Pahlavi and Farah Diba in Finland" by Markku Lepola. From Journalistic Picture Archive JOKA, Markku Lepola's collection. This image is licensed under CC BY 4.0. Retrieved from: https://www.finna.fi/Record/museovirasto.16EEB3744 D99CF345B79D1449180CA55.

They noted that there were new generations of jihadists who were prepared to fight against US dominance to their death. But these groups could not expect sustained support from any Islamic state and the US had little reason to fear them.

The US had also observed that Pakistan had followed India to acquire nuclear weapons. That did ring alarm bells in Washington. However, it soon saw how both the countries were careful to balance each other, however precariously, and neither power was likely to turn against the West. In any case, the Indic civilisation in India was still struggling to develop its economy and was not in any condition to challenge American supremacy. This then left the West with the homeland of Sinic civilisation, the PRC.

The global struggle between the US and the PRC today has become everyone's daily fare. How did that happen? The subject has been large enough for debates in numerous conferences and workshops and indeed many volumes by experts have been published. This is not the place even for its outlines to be adequately covered. I shall therefore limit myself to a brief survey of the civilisational and cultural factors that have surfaced, notably where they could be related to what Southeast Asian nation-states would now have to face.

I had earlier outlined how imperial America had offered China the gentler face of Western civilisation before the CCP defeated nationalist ROC in 1949. That changed when Mao Zedong sided with the Soviet Union and the US did everything it could to stop the PRC from taking its place as China in the UN. In time, it saw how Maoist China was alienated from Russia and successfully detached it from the Soviet bloc. The Cultural Revolution drew attention to civilisational differences the PRC now had with both the NATO West and the Soviets, and these differences contributed to undermining Chinese efforts to industrialise its economy. The CCP thus learnt a hard lesson, and after Mao Zedong's death, Deng Xiaoping reversed all of his policies.

The Chinese people were delighted to see the country connect with the free market capitalism that had globalised the world afresh and readily opened their colleges and universities to all scientific knowledge. The dramatic changes in productivity and the success of market reforms were breathtaking. In contrast, the Soviet economy was sputtering. The Russian leadership faltered and the Soviet Union's collapse became inevitable. As the Chinese saw it, their success had come from civilisational capacities that had drawn on deep historical roots.

When the Cold War ended and a triumphant US was poised to lead the world, the two faces of the Enlightenment Modern resurfaced. Its liberal face hardened as the superpower set out to ensure that there would never again be a serious challenger to its dominance. Looking around, all was reassuring, especially when China's reformists seemed prepared to abandon their Maoist past and learn from the US experience.

Figure 8. PRC Senior Vice-Premier Deng Xiaoping Signing a Guestbook During His Visit to Singapore (1978)

Source: Ministry of Information and the Arts Collection, courtesy of National Archives of Singapore.

That optimism came to a halt when the Tiananmen demonstrations led to a bloody end and both the US and Chinese leaders had to turn to their cultural backgrounds afresh. This included a review of each country's national interests. Both observed how the Soviet Union broke up into more than a dozen independent nation-states. US strategists worked on the scenarios that could follow. President Clinton was briefed that, unlike the Islamic and the Indic, the Sinic civilisation in China was founded on a unitary imperial system. It was now also a sovereign modern state of many nationalities. After two revolutions, Chinese nationalist and communist leaders had gone a long way to replace their ancient traditions with the Enlightenment Modern. But both groups had ambitions to rejuvenate their civilisation.

Americans placed their faith in the Enlightenment civilisation that hinged on social and cultural mobility. They hoped that the success of capitalism would produce a middle class that could bring China to liberal democracy. Although that has not happened, that faith was not as naïve as what is being depicted today. Many PRC officials and intellectuals were persuaded of the merits of greater freedom for a national revival. A greater degree of freedom would not only inspire capable entrepreneurs, but also the scientists and engineers who would ensure that someday the PRC would become the world's leading economy.

When a confident US set out to transform the Middle East by attacking Iraq and Afghanistan, Chinese leaders supported its war against terrorism and concentrated on establishing Chinese socialism with carefully selected capitalist institutions. They expected their success to demonstrate that China was not an ancient civilisation trying to modernise. They had succeeded in using Enlightenment modernity to re-connect with the country's unbroken history as a strong centralised state. By sifting out the liberal values of the Modern that hampered their efforts to build a sovereign state, they could eventually combine the new Enlightenment with the exceptional Sinic vision of *tianxia* as a civilisation-state.

The US acting as the guardian of modern civilisation was also akin to a civilisation-state. When it was confident that only its values were universal, it could look at China's ambitions without fear. However, after their failures in the Middle East, there was growing alarm. Watching the PRC emerge like a civilisation-state being rebuilt as a party-nation, the US began to see a possible threat to its global hegemony as well as its leadership of the civilised world. The possibility of that happening led it to round up its allies to contain the PRC or, if necessary, destroy the model altogether.

The ideological portrayal of China as a replica of the evil Leninist Russia is the main thrust in international discourse. It gained further emphasis when Taiwan and the South China Sea became the centre of attention. Both the ROC and the PRC administer some islands in the South China Sea. The PRC claimed to have inherited the dotted lines that the ROC in 1947 had drawn on maps of the sea. That placed half the Southeast Asian nation-states on the frontline of a disputed zone. Later on, new energy resources were

Figure 9. South China Sea Claims and Boundary Agreements (2012)

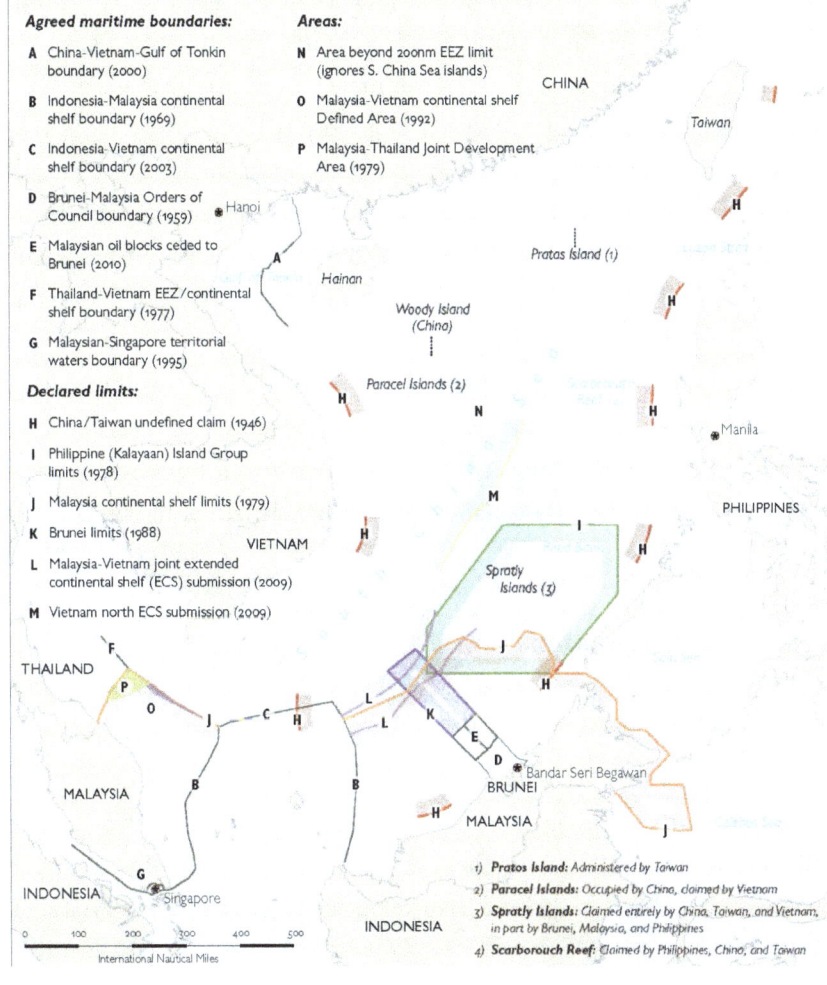

Source: US Department of Defense's Annual Report on China to Congress, 2012. Retrieved from: https://dod.defense.gov/Portals/1/Documents/pubs/2012_CMPR_Final.pdf.
The appearance of US Department of Defense (DoD) visual information does not imply or constitute DoD endorsement.

identified and all claimants have militarised several of the islands to protect their claims. Furthermore, the US insisted that the sea was open, international water and regularly sailed its naval forces to support its claim to protect Taiwan and the region from Chinese bullying.

The PRC, however, saw the South China Sea as the weak backyard that had made China vulnerable to hostile attacks. The sea is also its gateway to the rest of the maritime world and is now its economic lifeline. As for Taiwan, the US has focused on whatever makes Taiwan appear as a de facto independent state and appears ready to go to war if the PRC tries to take back the island by force. Whether all action was couched in terms of "America first" or "China first", both powers have shifted their position from civilisational competition to calls for the gathering of allies and partners, as well as for the best possible weaponry in defense of nationalist interests. Together, the prospects for dangerous conflict could not be more uncertain. I hope that security experts and political leaders will find ways to keep the peace. My only regret is that the superpowers concerned have moved away from the idea that civilisations could be winsome and borderless to concentrate on nationalist cultures that could increase the danger to world peace.

Living With Civilisations

Our region began as a large peninsula developed by agrarian communities in river valleys, and it was linked to an archipelago of trading ports whose peoples moved freely across many seas. Both halves interacted deeply with an ancient Indic civilisation that remained influential for at least a millennium. After that, three other civilisations, the Islamic, the Sinic and the Christian European, helped to develop the region's local and national cultures. It was these cultures that faced the Enlightenment Modern imposed on them by Western national empires. They observed what the older civilisations did to modernise and also used their experiences of the colonial modern to help them build nation-states with new national borders. At the end of the Cold War, all 10 states came together as an enlarged ASEAN and learnt to deal with the globalised world as a regional association. However, their ties with other civilisations were retained largely through its mix of peoples who remained proud of their respective civilisations and helped to keep their plural societies alive.

In the development of ASEAN, the cultural responses of its members to modernisation are all founded on common aspirations to build nation-states. These cultural responses can be grouped as follows. For Indonesia, Malaysia and Brunei, the links with their Islamic *Ummah* have grown stronger. Similarly, the links of most Filipinos with their Christian and trans-Pacific co-religionists remain firm despite the distances involved. A common faith continues to connect Thailand, Myanmar, Laos and Cambodia to countries that have large numbers of Buddhist believers. As for Vietnam, it has retained its Sinic culture through a shared history of recent revolutions. And then there is Singapore with its majority of citizens of Chinese origins having obvious links with modern Sinic civilisation. It is encouraging to see how these groupings have not prevented the 10 nation-states from acting in their common interests whenever they needed to do so.

Singapore tells an extraordinary story of adjustment and adaptation that is especially pertinent to the subject of these lectures. As an unexpected nation-state, its first leaders did well by their decision to embrace its modern administrative and legal heritage and expand the range of its imperial economic connections. It saw the UN organisation as the embodiment of a renewed Enlightenment civilisation. This protected sovereign nation-states wherever located and however small. With this shield, the island-state was enabled to nation-build with a plural society that drew from several living civilisations. From a unique combination of policies and practices, the new state laid the foundations of a first world nation at the heart of Southeast Asia.

Everyone was conscious that three-quarters of Singapore's population was of Chinese origins. That had always been a source of unease in the region. Furthermore, no one foresaw the swift rise of the PRC and its turn towards a state-centred capitalism that provided it with the economic power to make it appear as a threat to the US. Nobody anticipated that the severely weakened Sinic civilisation could have used its two revolutions to achieve modernisation so quickly. It now claimed to be the successor to a continuous

Sinic centralised state. When China also claimed to have drawn inspiration from the same Enlightenment roots as the West, the US began to demonise the CCP-led party-state as returning to the ideology previously represented by the Soviet Union. This ignores China's deep roots in a civilisation that had considered itself central and exceptional for millennia.

China's success in using the developed world's free market economy to reach out to the developing world has made its modern claims more credible than anyone thought possible. Equally surprising has been the American response. Politically polarised by extremists of every colour and creed, the US has called for an aggressive nationalism against the PRC. That seemed to have been the only call that could unite the country. In response, China has revived the nationalism that had enabled its people to resist Japanese invasions a century earlier. What is new is that both the PRC and the US now see themselves as representatives of progressive civilisations. The US as guardian of the liberal Enlightenment has portrayed the PRC as a throwback to the failed ideology of communism. It has now asked for its military allies in NATO to move further east to help end the threat of a rerun. Together, they hope to restore the liberal dominance that had triumphantly won the Cold War.

I cannot predict the outcome of that dangerous rivalry. The uncertainty is likely to stay. Where Singapore in Southeast Asia is concerned, I am one of many who have been concerned as to what those of Chinese origins might do when the PRC calls on them as Chinese to sympathise with its aspirations for the future. Needless to say, there will also be repercussions in other ASEAN states. But no other state has a majority whose populace might be expected to provide a singular response to this inescapable dilemma.

Given Southeast Asia's history of local cultures selecting what they needed from the civilisations they encountered, Singapore's best interest seems to be to support the common aspirations of all member states of our region. What it could do is to remind the new nation-states of their experiences with civilisations in the past, and the way they grew their local cultures by dealing with and learning from neighbouring civilisations. What they had chosen to learn were qualities that were borderless, those not identified with any national political system. Having done that for centuries, each ASEAN member had become confident in dealing with unpredictable conditions. In that way, each has been able to strengthen its local cultures and shape its own modern national culture. This was why the nation-states were able to come together and stay united as ASEAN when it was in their combined interests to do so.

Singapore as a state has chosen to stay with this common experience. It is committed to the idea that its citizens of whatever origin should respond only to borderless civilisational appeals and not to nationalist ones. At its simplest where the PRC is concerned, it could distinguish between the current national culture and timeless Sinic civilisation. In Chinese, this would recognise a difference between *zhongguo wenhua* (中国文化) and *zhonghua wenming* (中华文明). China today has them both and may not think it necessary or important to project them separately. Singapore's modern culture would require its leaders to try their hardest to keep the national and the civilisational clearly differentiated.

I do not want to give the impression that this would be easy to do. Careful judgements would have to be consistently made and many cultural specialists would have to be involved to distinguish the two. But if successfully done, it should produce results that avoid any misunderstanding for all concerned. The most important contribution of this differentiation is to ensure that Singaporeans of Chinese origin would be able to act in ways that the whole ASEAN community can understand and be comfortable with. That would show how a modern nation-state could, as with cultures in the past, co-exist with a variety of living civilisations.

There is no question that all ASEAN states will closely observe how Singapore resolves its exceptional conundrum. The modernity with which the nation-states have identified should provide each of them with the capacity to deal with social plurality, although the scale of each manifestation is different. Furthermore, if Singapore can sort out its problems with its citizenry and show how that response conforms to Southeast Asian experiences, it should strengthen the region's confidence in responding to its relations with other civilisations. The region is fortunate to be one that is both maritime and continental and also located strategically between two oceans that are vital to global prosperity. If it can hold firm as a united ASEAN that co-exists with living civilisations, that might help to prevent our peace-seeking multi-civilisational world from descending into the warring nationalist cultures that threaten us today.

Question-and-Answer Session
Moderated by Mr Bilahari Kausikan

Mr Bilahari Kausikan: Thank you, Prof Wang, that was truly breathtaking. Ladies and gentlemen, I think you will agree with me that Prof Wang's S R Nathan lectures are unique in this entire series of lectures. I don't think any previous set of lectures has had quite the range and broad sweep, nor have they been animated with such subtle but brave concepts. The result is a philosophic study of history in its true sense, where you have broad concepts allied to the facts in which history must be grounded.

I think this has been unique also in giving us a valuable background to some of the contemporary problems that we face. I'm not just talking about the geopolitical rivalry between the US and China. Of course that has cast its shadow over almost every aspect of international life today, and I think it has become a structural condition of international relations for the foreseeable future. But more essentially and more immediately for us is what you have just heard in the last part of this lecture, which is something I think a number of us have been grappling with, but without the erudition and depth of knowledge of Prof Wang.

Prof Wang is truly unique. I was tempted to call him a living national treasure. However, that seems too narrow. Perhaps I could call him a living civilisational force or intellectual force — a living civilisational force that we are fortunate to have here in Singapore, at least for now, because civilisations know no boundaries as we have just heard. I was going to exercise my moderator's privilege to ask the first question, but having listened to the lecture, I need some time to collect my own thoughts to ask an intelligent question. I will start by opening the floor to the audience and I may come back later with my own question.

Participant: I wonder if you could comment on two particular examples in Southeast Asia. First, there is the coup d'état in Myanmar and second, the Chinese behaviour in the South China Sea. Do these two examples illustrate the weakness of ASEAN — perhaps its fatal weakness?

Prof Wang: These are examples of the tests that ASEAN has been facing for many years. In fact, ASEAN has never had things easy from the very beginning, and Myanmar certainly is an extraordinary problem. In a sense if you look back, it all stems from our region's difficulty with the whole idea of building nation-states. As I've said earlier on, nation-states were a totally new concept to this part of the world. We had kingdoms, sultanates, rajahs and all kinds of feudal and dynastic states in the past, but nation-states were totally new. I think the region has done very well to adapt itself to the fact that there were many plural societies under different kinds of rulers who shaped our nation-states. In that respect, we've done reasonably well.

We should also bear in mind that all the Southeast Asian countries started with borders we didn't draw by ourselves. All the national borders of the ASEAN states were drawn by somebody else and we were left carrying the baby, so to speak, to try and make something of it and nation-build. Our efforts from that point of view have been enormously successful in my mind. Much more successful than anyone anticipated, even though I would say that all the ASEAN states face serious problems and these nations are still work in progress. Myanmar is probably the worst of all the 10 examples that we have.

The national borders of the ASEAN states were drawn by colonisers. There are so many ethnic groups within these borders, and these are not small, simple groups but large ethnic groups with their own traditions and cultures. They were all pulled together into this map of Burma, which was then left to the Union of Burma when it became independent. There was the hope that somehow the newly independent Burma would become united and find new ways of compromising to establish a nation-state. But from the very beginning, it was not the nature of the Burmese culture of that time — the national culture of their military in particular — to compromise and find a solution. So I think we're now facing the biggest test of our region with regards to the coup d'état in Myanmar. How can we survive this? I'm by no means optimistic about the answer. We will find a compromise somehow but it will not be one that will make anybody happy, I regret to say.

For your second example on the South China Sea — again there are so many complicated issues involved. Fundamentally, it is this: China has never had enemies coming by sea in the past. Only in the last 150 years did they realise that they were vulnerable at sea. Out of their 3,000 years of history, they've never had enemies by sea. However, in the 19th century, China realised that it could be attacked by sea, so it has become very defensive in its attitude. In the past, China had always been defensive up in the north because of overland enemies from Central Asia. Till today, they remain sensitive. China is good at handling Central Asian and overland continental matters. But maritime matters are new to them. They've never known the meaning of a sea border, and I'm not sure anybody knew what those 11 dotted lines (which they started with) meant when they were first drawn up in the South China Sea. I don't know if anybody understood that. The PRC as they see it inherited those claims. They didn't actually draw the dash lines as well. Incidentally, as you all know, it was drawn by the ROC, and I think when the lines were drawn, the party was still very active as nationalist China and a close ally of the US, and they were all aware of those lines being drawn.

As a school boy, I remember maps of China in 1947 that already had those dotted lines drawn in. They were already there, and the communists, known as the PRC, took over that map. They believed that they inherited the dotted lines in the South China Sea, and therefore must defend it. This is the map of China that's part of their sovereignty and that came with their legitimacy as victors of the battlefield. China has reiterated this recently as well. Qin Gang, China's former Minister of Foreign Affairs, particularly re-emphasised again the red line (the nine-dash line) which should not be crossed, and that's how seriously they're prepared to go to war about the issue. But whether they will go to war on their own or whether they will go to war only because they are provoked to war, I do not know. That's a different story. This issue has now been overtaken by the US–China competition in a way that has nothing to do with the more abstract or legal ideas of what sovereignty means.

Participant: I've been listening to your old lectures and I'm really fascinated with your ideas about civilisation and culture. I'd like to ask about how they might apply to a broader view of history, because I've been very interested in decolonial theory as written about by Walter Mignolo and others. He's challenging this whole idea of Christian Enlightenment modernity by drawing ideas centered on indigenous cultures of the Americas, or Africa.

Also, in a more regional context, people are trying to do similar things with the Orang Laut or Orang Asli ways of thinking. So I was wondering, would you say there is a possibility of building civilisational ideas in the future from cultures which didn't start off as urban or literate? Is it possible to build up these civilisations of the future based on say, indigenous American or maritime Southeast Asian thinking?

Prof Wang: It's a question that I did try to answer in my earlier lectures. I have found those two words (culture and civilisation) extremely confusing in their uses by various people in the arguments, both in historical as well as political and cultural writings. So, I have tried to distinguish between them to try and make it very clear that there is a difference between the two.

The thing about it is that everybody has cultures, including all the indigenous groups. Every group has cultures, from the most primitive ones to the large cultures that are represented by big countries like the US, China, Japan or India. Everybody can have cultures, but civilisation is something different. Civilisation is something that doesn't belong to any particular nation and the quality that distinguishes it from cultures is that it is borderless. It represents certain qualities of thinking, of behaving, of how human beings should see their past, future and present. That actually transcends borders — this quality distinguishes civilisations from nations, cultures and tribes, and once you separate them, you can see that there were many attempts to build civilisations in the past. Many of them failed and died out. Now, there are only four or five that are still living civilisations as per my definition. These are still civilisations that offer everything to anybody who wants to take the best of them and make what they like of them. These civilisations include Enlightenment civilisation as well as the Indic, Sinic, Islamic and Christian European. They all offer something that is beyond borders, and because they are good in themselves, they are attractive and others draw from them, taking what they want. So, there are no boundaries on what one should and should not take. The moment there are barriers on what should and should not be taken, that already crosses the line into something else more judgemental.

But the civilisations that exist today stand for something more than just cultures, nationalities or tribes, and so cultures will draw from different civilisations that enable them to develop in various different ways. Each of these cultures should be respected for what they are, but they are not the same as civilisations. The moment you claim to say you represent a civilisation, and claim to determine what is civilising and what is not, then you are creating a new kind of framework. But to me, the moment you have to do that — that is no longer a civilisation. So, when a country says that they are a leader in a certain aspect, or that others ought to be behaving differently, that's not civilisation. That kind of metric is not civilisational. That is culture, a dominant, hegemonic culture.

Participant: You mentioned that there was concern where societies with large Chinese populations would be pressured to sympathise with China. Similarly, there were previously the same concerns for the Malay community. There were policies that were put in place to ensure that Singapore remains secure. So now that you've brought up this issue of the Chinese population, where do you see Singapore putting policies in place to ensure security, should these things happen?

Prof Wang: Well the government has enacted so many policies I can't go into all of them. They have been very sensitive from the beginning to the reality of the large Chinese population. To add on, this issue was seen not just in Singapore. The Chinese "problem" as they call it, was already a sensitive one in the whole region. So, the government of Singapore was sensitive to it from day one and they've been trying to work out different ways to deal with it. And as I said, not all measures have succeeded, but on the whole, they got the right idea. They recognise the importance of a plural society, where one cannot tell someone to stop being Malay, Indian or Chinese. That's nonsensical. If you believe in the concept of a plural society, then everyone is equal in the eyes of the state. What you want to do is to say that everyone belongs to the plural society of Singapore. It will develop its national culture based on this particular mix of plurality in Singapore. You can still love and respect your civilisational roots and the things that make you Chinese, Malay or Indian. That is perfectly fine as long as you distinguish them very clearly from the national interests of those countries that claim that civilisation. That's a different matter. That is national culture, so at least by using cultures and civilisations differently and separately, I hope it makes this differentiation a bit easier.

It's not going to be easy to differentiate between the two. It's not easy and the government has been trying to achieve this. They have been struggling with it over the decades and the people within Singapore, including Chinese people themselves, have not always understood this need for separation between civilisational and national calls. Not all have been happy with what the government is doing, but this struggle goes on and the attention will remain. But as long as it is clear in everybody's mind that you can differentiate between a civilisation and a national culture, then there is a chance.

For example, if you say that you love Chinese poetry, calligraphy, art, music or even Chinese food, these have nothing to do with governments and nationalities anywhere. You can do what you like. But if the Chinese Government begins to dictate what people should eat, listen to or enjoy, one would immediately be able to tell that they have been forced to like something. We love what we do because of its quality, of course. For example, to me, the most beautiful thing about Indian civilisation is their theatre, their drama and their dance. The kind of dance and music that the Indian civilisation has represented through the centuries is absolutely unique and that is something that is borderless which everybody can appreciate. In fact, many civilisations have drawn inspiration from that source. And you recognise it did come from India, from Indic civilisation. However, it's not part of the Indian Government. This is just to highlight and contrast the two terms I have been discussing.

Participant: Your lecture made me think of traditional ways to live adopted by various cultures set against the modern civilisation that we are seeing in Singapore. This is especially important since we are seeing more immigrants who are coming to Singapore to work and learn, and who are being retained here in Singapore.

How can the modern civilisation as you pointed out influence the Sustainable Development Goals by the UN? Is it going to revise these goals and should it enforce others to follow this code of practice? Because Singapore places emphasis on going global, but when we are cultivated and motivated from Singapore, it could be restricting us from exploring globally. However, if the UN could revise these goals, and Singapore implements them, perhaps Singapore could be made more international and global. Your views?

Prof Wang: The ramifications of those questions are very great. It reminds me to say that this is not a single problem that stays still and can be solved quickly. It is a moving target. For example, we now talk about the

Singaporean population actually shrinking in relation to the total population, and about how we're having new migrants who have to adjust to a Singapore condition. That will continue. I don't expect that to change.

Singaporeans have global aspirations and at the same time, Singaporeans are also tremendously locked into their own local interest. The things that Singaporeans love and long for when they're away from home are very clear. We do have that measure. So, there are many levels to this issue, and on each level, there are different operations concerned. But when you have new migrants coming in, obviously they are bringing with them their own civilisational and cultural values. And what they have to do is to try and adjust themselves and adapt themselves to Singaporean ways. Now this is not going to be a straightforward matter. It's something that needs continual attention, which is why I said I'm not suggesting this is at all easy. It is something that you have to continually watch out for and deal with, particularly because these issues and circumstances are changing all the time.

In fact, quite frankly I've said this before, I deeply regret the pace at which changes take place today. When I was young, things moved very slowly. I had time to think about what was going to happen and so on. Nowadays, there's something happening every day. I no longer can keep up. So, I greatly regret the speed of things that are happening now. That very speed affects the same question that I'm raising today. The fact is that all these new elements require speedy attention. Not only deep attention, but also speedy attention. So, unless you have the principles clear in your own mind, speedy reactions could lead to bad mistakes. If actions are not thought through, and long-term factors are not considered, we are quite likely to make very bad mistakes. So this question of having to adjust oneself even according to time constraints is something that I wish I didn't have to see in my lifetime — to see myself so helpless in the face of all these rapid changes that are happening around me. When I look at what young Singaporeans are studying today, I don't even understand the first step of what they are doing. As such, I'm not sure what I can say about the future.

You can see why I say there are limits to what I can even imagine, so please bear that in mind too.

Mr Kausikan: I'll take one of the online questions first, which will bring the conversation back to Asia. A participant asked a very specific question about Timor Leste and I'll summarise it. The addition of Timor Leste to ASEAN represents a redefinition of the idea of Southeast Asia. What do you think of this? Is this a wise move or a bridge too far?

Prof Wang: I think this is not a cultural or civilisation problem. It's a policy problem on the part of the government and I think that for various reasons. It may be in the interests of the 10 ASEAN states to include Timor Leste. If they have a specific reason for this, I would say that it is not a general question. It is a very specific question and can only be settled by a specific set of answers concerned with immediate interests of the region.

Mr Kausikan: Actually, only time will tell.

Participant: Earlier on, you mentioned the concerns that people have about large Chinese populations in Southeast Asia. In Thailand where they have one of the largest overseas Chinese populations, the Chinese seem to have assimilated and integrated quite well into Thailand. Do you foresee a time when Singaporean Chinese would be seen as so well-integrated into Singapore and Southeast Asia where this current issue would be less of a concern?

Prof Wang: The government of all the countries in ASEAN have very careful policies about what they want with regards to the issue. Thailand has been as you described — almost seamlessly evolved for centuries. The country has actually in a way been like this because it was never colonised. The Thai elites were allowed to play a bigger role in defining what it means to be Thai and they have succeeded in extraordinary ways. I would say that the vast majority of those who call themselves Sino-Thai are so Thai that it is hard for them to even prove that they are Chinese, which may be perfectly natural. The fact that they still see themselves (if at all) as Sino-Thai is simply an example of affectionate memory. There's no political significance.

So again, the words "culture" and "civilisation" come back. The word "culture" has boundaries, and is defined by nation-states and what a country considers its national interest. Once you take these national interests into concern, then the people in that country must adapt and adjust accordingly to make sure that stability and order in that country is preserved. Who knows how long it will be before Singapore reaches the condition of Thailand? I do not know. It sounds like a very long time from now because Singapore did not start out in the same position.

Thailand started out with a population that was 100 per cent Thai, before Chinese people came in. It took a long time to reach this present position where there are so many people of Chinese descent in Thailand. Singapore started out the other way around. We had a population that was 75 per cent Chinese, and the whole society and government are trying very hard to keep some of the racial ratios, so they don't have to change fundamental things in the system. So there are many other underlying factors to consider regarding the Chinese population, such as whether it affects housing and jobs or the selection of people who should fulfil specific ratios. All these things are happening every day and I think these will probably continue for a long time.

Participant: You mentioned previously that China prefers a united ASEAN, but that this united ASEAN must be pro-China and not against China. Recently Mr Kausikan also mentioned that although the US and China both say that they will not push ASEAN to take sides, both countries are in fact doing that.

Today, China is still mainly a continental superpower and the US is mainly a maritime superpower. As such, the disputes and clashes between them are actually dividing ASEAN. So, my question is this: Can you assess the possibility or risk of ASEAN being divided into continental ASEAN and maritime ASEAN in the future because of this rivalry?

Prof Wang: That is a very specific question. Let me first say that for your general question on the possibility of China and the US dividing ASEAN, I'll be a very powerful person if I knew the answer. All the governments would be inviting me to be adviser to them to solve the problem. I don't have the answer to that one. In fact, I'm not sure anybody does. It is pointless for me to speculate here.

However, on your specific question about continental and maritime Southeast Asia, I think that is an interesting question. ASEAN did actually overcome that a long while ago, as early as the 1990s, when they broke away from this idea of the original ASEAN which was basically maritime. They did this by bringing the continental side of it together as well. What is so remarkable is that ever since 1999, in the last 20 years, the ASEAN states have overcome a lot of their differences even when they didn't understand the other parties. An example is the differences between the maritime and the continental states. A few of these differences have come up in some of the discussions going on.

They have managed to stay together, based on this key point: What are their common interests? ASEAN needs to recognise that their common interest is to stay together, because if they separate, they become vassals or just client states of whoever the power is. In this case, I would say continental or maritime would not matter all that much, and the importance of staying together is more important. Ultimately, it's the survival of a sense of a region which interestingly enough, did not have a name and was not self-conscious before 1945. Since then, all the efforts made to draw this picture of a region have been remarkably successful. All the elites in the 10 countries are perfectly aware of this and they have all come to more or less different degrees of certainty that it is the common interest of all 10 states to stay together somehow. They might change their stances a little as the situation demands, but always with the same goal in mind. This goal is that the region should be kept as a region that can play a part globally as a whole. And it can only play a part if it stays a united region. I think that's the only way I can see it.

Participant: This is more of a comment than a question. I previously observed a few school groups that were doing heritage tours and I found them very mono-directional and slightly ritualistic. It's hard for me to see how the students were engaging with the materials, and as you mentioned, it should be an exchange between culturalists and historians to determine the culture that we want to pass on to our future generations. However, all these are just external scaffoldings. What do you think are the internal architecture that we should teach our children to have? Because at the end of the day, we also want to have active discussions about where and how people can live their heritage.

Prof Wang: I think it's not going to be a simple answer but I think the idea that you live your heritage is a good way of describing it — that you could do that because you identify with a civilisation with no borders. It has something to do with people internalising this identity within themselves, or from their family and those akin to them who share their interests. And what these groups have in common keeps them together and they have a shared heritage. But that heritage has no political implications. It's not defined by national interests. It is entirely defined by their own cultural leanings and as well as their desires to retain what they believe to be beautiful and which they respect. Nobody should prevent them from doing so because these values are meant to be borderless.

A perfect example of this would be things like scientific knowledge, technological knowledge or economic knowledge. They're borderless, and everybody can learn them. If you learn them, you apply it to whatever you need to do. No nation can claim that this knowledge is entirely their own and they cannot tell others not to learn it. This has nothing to do with national interest. National interest relates to nation-states, and it is important to note that under the UN, all nation-states are equal in status. In fact, although it might not be the case today, the concept of all states under the UN being equal was a marvellous idea. All states are equal in status in that organisation, but it is difficult to achieve. In fact, it might not be achievable in the long run, but the effort to achieve it is something that we must keep fighting for. That's national interest. But civilisationally, we should be able to learn from everyone, as long as something attracts us. And this has nothing to do with national interests. We should be able to learn from civilisations because they are so appealing that we don't care where the idea comes from.

Mr Kausikan: I'm going to hijack one of the online questions and recast it as my own. Mr Vladimir Putin has justified his war against Ukraine in civilisational terms. Whether you believe it or not, this is his justification. How do you think it has or has not affected how China looks at its own civilisational identity and its interests? Has it learned things to do or things not to do?

Prof Wang: I think my answer is that there's a big difference between what Putin's idea of civilisational terms is and what China's idea is. Putin's idea is actually based on the last 200 years of Enlightenment Modern history in Europe when nation-states were created. National empires were created and they disagreed on very fundamental values regarding freedom of capitalism and the freedom to redistribute wealth to the poor and the workers. There are differences even within every society but these views (capitalist and communist) have been ideologically presented as opposites and that is how Putin still sees it. And in those terms, his civilisational terms are still couched in that European context of disagreeing about the ideological nature of society. The society that is open to capitalism in the way the rest of Europe is, right at the borders of Russia, was unacceptable to him. That is how he defined Russia's civilisational view. So, it's a very narrow civilisational concern.

The Chinese civilisational view is actually not free for the Chinese to choose. They've inherited 3,000 years of history and they look at their history with great love and concern. They draw on the history for almost everything, and it has shaped what they believe in. They do believe in the continuity of their 3,000 years of history, as well as the successes of China's rises and falls. China has been conquered by so many people, but in the end, the civilisation survived all the conquests. The civilisation fell and rose again and this has given the Chinese a sense of civilisational continuity, which now has been strengthened by a belief in the future which I spoke on previously. This then turned into a belief in the idea of progress, which is something that the Chinese never believed in the past. Before, all they hoped for was to recover, to reinvent themselves continually within the context of the old ancient Chinese civilisation, while renewing it from time to time.

However, now they actually believe in the idea of progress. This refers to the material progress that improves constantly and is developed by science and technology, entrepreneurship, economic and financial development, and which they learned from the West. They don't hide the fact that they learned this idea of progress from the West. They have acknowledged that they have taken what they felt was useful from the West, while not incorporating what they thought was not so useful. It so happens that the Americans have looked at what the Chinese did not copy from them, and set that as a benchmark to judge their civilisation. This is also what the Chinese and Americans disputed over, and it's a dispute which is civilisational and for which I can find no answer. How can you satisfy both sides on a matter like that?

Mr Kausikan: And on that very optimistic note, we shall have to stop now. Please join me in thanking Prof Wang.

Afterword

When reviewing my text for publication, I noted that the last section of my fourth lecture dealt with Chinese culture and civilisation only in the context of people of Chinese descent who have settled outside China and become foreign nationals. In particular, I paid special attention to the position of Singapore's ethnic Chinese majority. I kept the reference simple by referring to the difference between how Singaporean Chinese might see *zhongguo wenhua* (中国文化) as the culture of the Chinese nation, and *zhonghua wenming* (中华文明) as Sinic civilisation.

This might have left unclear how the culture–civilisation distinction is played out more generally with regard to the condition of Sinic civilisation today as compared with the culture of the Chinese nation-state. I gave thought to adding a couple of paragraphs to the lecture to cover this issue, but realised that would distract from the focus on Southeast Asia that brought the lectures to a conclusion. I also considered providing a fuller explanation of the Sinic connection as a footnote but thought that would not be adequate. So, I decided to leave the lecture unchanged.

After a final look at the manuscript before sending it to the printers, I saw that an Afterword should be provided to explain how Sinic civilisation followed its own trajectory of change to become something that might be called a civilisation-state among the neighbouring states it most influenced. As it happened over several centuries, a group of states — most notably Korea, Vietnam and Japan — had accepted Sinic civilisation as a frame of reference with values and institutions that enriched their local cultures. When China became identified with the Qin-Han Empire that classified other states as tributary states, or *chaogongguo* (朝贡国), it stood at the head of its *tianxia* (天下), or all-under-heaven system.

During the 19th century, this system was challenged by the Enlightenment nation-state empires. It had to be abandoned when the "tributary states" became European colonies, notably Vietnam under the French. At the same time, Japan as a state that had chosen to use many

Sinic institutions without paying tribute to China was quick to see the advantage of adopting key features of modern civilisation brought to Asia by the Western powers. Meiji Japan was militarised to defeat the Qing Empire and turn Korea into its colony. This in turn inspired Han Chinese revolutionaries to turn against Manchu rule. When the Republic of China inherited the Qing imperial borders, the nationalists established the *zhonghua minguo* (中华民国) as a multi-national sovereign state.

Insofar as Sinic civilisation became part of the cultures of Korea, Vietnam and Japan, it remained borderless. But where it was claimed as foundational tradition by the Chinese state, that made the ancient civilisation part of the republic's national culture. That did not make it necessary for people in China to differentiate between their culture and their civilisation. However, for the non-Chinese, that separation became normal. To take a few examples, we know that Korean Confucians, Vietnamese Daoists and Japanese Mahayana Buddhists could continue to identify with some sacred places in China and visit them regularly without affecting their sense of national identity. And descendants of *waiji huaren* (外籍华人), or Chinese with foreign passports, could do the same if they wished. Their respect and admiration for Sinic traditions could be quite distinct from their loyalty to their respective countries. It could also be clearly separated from their dealings with China as a nation-state.

The Sinic civilisation I have outlined above has regained fresh attention together with the living Indic, Islamic and Enlightenment Christian civilisations that co-exist in the world today. All have been empowered by the modern–ancient confrontations of the past two centuries. No less important, scores of national cultures have sought to develop beyond their borders. And a regional coalescence phenomenon may yet emerge to further diversify the nature of the international community. I believe that nation-states, regions and the world order will all benefit if enough respect is given to the civilisations that have survived numerous calamities and enriched humanity through the ages. This has encouraged me to end with the following lines.

Heaven earth and man no borders need
unruly tribes and nations really do.
Harbouring cultures can only do so much
when civilisations are left to die.

Moderns began to slay the ancients
slitting multitudes of veins instead.
Living peoples pave their highways
to peaceful heavens with teachings better read.

Selected Bibliography

Abdullah, Firdaus Haji. *Radical Malay Politics: Its Origins and Early Development.* Petaling Jaya: Pelanduk Publications, 1985.

Acharya, Amitav. *Civilizations in Embrace: The Spread of Ideas and the Transformation of Power: India and Southeast Asia in the Classical Age.* Singapore: Institute of Southeast Asian Studies, 2013.

Acri, Andrea, and Peter Sharrock. *The Creative South — Vol. 1: Buddhist and Hindu Art in Medieval Maritime Asia; Vol. 2: Odisha and Java.* Singapore: ISEAS-Yusof Ishak Institute, 2022.

Alatas, Syed Farid. *Democracy and Authoritarianism in Indonesia and Malaysia: The Rise of the Post-Colonial State.* New York: St Martin's Press, 1997.

Alatas, Syed Hussein. *The Myth of the Lazy Native: A Study of the Image of the Malays, Filipinos and Javanese from the 16th to the 20th Century and its Function in the Ideology of Colonial Capitalism.* London: Frank Cass, 1977.

Alishahbana, S. Takdir. *Indonesia: Social and Cultural Revolution.* Translated by Benedict Anderson. Kuala Lumpur: Oxford University Press, 1966.

Amyot, Jacques. *The Manila Chinese: Familism in the Philippine Environment.* Manila: Institute of Philippine Culture, 1973.

Andaya, Leonard. *Leaves from the Same Tree: Trade and Ethnicity in the Straits of Malacca.* Honolulu: University of Hawaii Press, 2008.

Anderson, Benedict. *Imagined Communities: Reflections on the Origin and Spread of Nationalism.* London: Verso Editions and New Left Books, 1983.

Anderson, Benedict. *Language and Power: Exploring Political Cultures in Indonesia.* New York: Cornell University Press, 1990.

Anderson, Benedict. *The Spectre of Comparisons: Nationalism, Southeast Asia and the World.* London: Verso, 1998.

Anwar, Zainah. *Islamic Revivalism in Malaysia.* Petaling Jaya: Pelanduk Publications, 1987.

Arasaratnam, Sinnappah. *Indians in Malaysia and Singapore.* Kuala Lumpur: Oxford University Press, 1970.

Arasaratnam, Sinnappah. *Maritime Trade, Society and European Influence in Southern Asia, 1600–1800.* Ashgate: Variorum, 1995.

Armstrong, M. Jocelyn. *Chinese Populations in Contemporary Southeast Asian Societies: Identities, Interdependence and International Influence.* Surrey, England: Curzon Press, 2001.

Atwill, David G. *The Chinese Sultanate: Islam, Ethnicity, and the Panthay Rebellion in Southwest China, 1856–1873.* Stanford: Stanford University Press, 2005.

Avari, Burjor. *Islamic Civilization in South Asia: A History of Muslim Power and Presence in the Indian Subcontinent.* London: Routledge, 2013.

Aydin, Cemil. *The Politics of Anti-Westernism in Asia: Visions of World Order in Pan-Islamic and Pan-Asian Thought.* New York: Columbia University Press, 2007.

Azra, Azyumardi. *The Origins of Islamic Reformism in Southeast Asia: Networks of Malay-Indonesian and Middle Eastern "Ulama" in the 17th and 18th centuries.* Honolulu: University of Hawaii Press, 2004.

Backus, Charles. *The Nan-chao Kingdom and T'ang China's Southwestern Frontier.* Cambridge: Cambridge University Press, 1981.

Bagchi, Prabodh Chandra. *India and China: Interactions Through Buddhism and Diplomacy: A Collection of Essays.* Compiled by Wang Bangwei and Tansen Sen. London: Anthem Press, 2011.

Barth, Frederik. *Ethnic Groups and Boundaries: The Social Organization of Culture Differences.* Boston: Little, Brown and Company, 1969.

Bayly, Christopher A. *Recovering Liberties: Indian Thought in the Age of Liberalism and Empire.* Cambridge: Cambridge University Press, 2011.

Befu, Harumi. *Cultural Nationalism in East Asia: Representation and Identity.* Berkeley: University of California Press, 1993.

Bellwood, Peter. *First Islanders: Prehistory and Human Migration in Island Southeast Asia.* Hoboken: Wiley Blackwell, 2017.

Benda, Harry J. *The Crescent and the Rising Sun: Indonesian Islam under the Japanese Occupation, 1942–1945.* The Hague and Bandung: Van Hoeve, 1958.

Benton, Gregor. *Chinese Indentured Labour in the Dutch East Indies, 1880–1942: Tin, Tobacco, Timber, and the Penal Sanction.* Cham: Palgrave Macmillan, 2022.

Bhabha, Homi K. *The Location of Culture.* London: Routledge, 1994.

Blusse, Leonard. *Strange Company: Chinese Settlers, Mestizo Women and the Dutch in VOC Batavia.* Dordrecht: KITLV Press, 1986.

Blythe, Wilfred L. *The Impact of Chinese Secret Societies in Malaya: A Historical Study.* Kuala Lumpur: Oxford University Press, 1969.

Bose, Sugata. *A Hundred Horizons: The Indian Ocean in the Age of Global Empire.* Cambridge: Harvard University Press, 2006.

Bowden, Brett. *The Empire of Civilization: The Evolution of an Imperial Idea.* Chicago: University of Chicago Press, 2009.

Braudel, Fernand. *A History of Civilizations.* Translated by Richard Mayne. New York: Penguin Book, 1993.

Braudel, Fernand. *The Mediterranean in the Ancient World.* Translated by Siân Reynolds. New York: Allen Lane, 2001.

Briggs, Lawrence Palmer. *The Ancient Khmer Empire.* Philadelphia: American Philosophical Society, 1951.

Brindley, Erica. *Ancient China and the Yue: Perceptions and Identities on the Southern Frontier, c.600 BCE–50 CE.* Cambridge: Cambridge University Press, 2015.

Budiman, Arief. *State and Civil Society in Indonesia.* Clayton: Centre for Southeast Asian Studies, Monash University, 1990.

Cantor, Norman F. *The Civilization of the Middle Ages: A Completely Revised and Expanded Edition of Medieval History, the Life and Death of a Civilization.* New York: Harper Perennial, 1994.

Carstens, Sharon. *Histories, Cultures, Identities: Studies in Malaysian Chinese Worlds.* Singapore: NUS Press, 2005.

Chakravarti, Nalini Ranjan. *The Indian Minority in Burma: The Rise and Decline of an Immigrant Community.* London: Oxford University Press, 1971.

Chaloemtiarana, Thak. *Thailand: The Politics of Despotic Paternalism.* Ithaca: Cornell University Press, 2007.

Chamoux, François. *Hellenistic Civilization.* Translated by Michel Roussel. Malden: Blackwell, 2003.

Chan, Heng Chee. *Singapore: The Politics of Survival, 1965–1967.* Kuala Lumpur: Oxford University Press, 1971.

Chandler, David P. *The Tragedy of Cambodian History: Politics, War and Revolution Since 1945.* New Haven: Yale University Press, 1991.

Chang, Hao. *Chinese Intellectuals in Crisis: Search for Order and Meaning (1890–1911).* Berkeley: University of California Press, 1987.

Chang, Sidney H., and Leonard H. D. Gordon. *All Under Heaven: Sun Yat-sen and his Revolutionary Thought.* Stanford: Hoover Institution Press, 1991.

Chang, T'ien-tse. *Sino-Portuguese Trade from 1514 to 1644.* Leiden: Brill, 1934.

Chapman, F. Spencer. *The Jungle is Neutral.* London: Chatto & Windus, 1949.

Chatterjee, Partha. *The Black Hole of Empire: History of a Global Practice of Power.* Princeton: Princeton University Press, 2012.

Chatterjee, Partha. *The Nation and Its Fragments: Colonial and Postcolonial Histories.* Princeton: Princeton University Press, 1994.

Chaudhuri, K. N. *Trade and Civilisation in the Indian Ocean: An Economic History from the Rise of Islam to 1750.* Cambridge: Cambridge University Press, 1985.

Cheah, Boon Kheng. *Red Star Over Malaya: Resistance and Social Conflict During and After the Japanese Occupation, 1941–1946.* Singapore: Singapore University Press, 1983.

Cheah, Boon Kheng. *The Masked Comrades: A Study of the Communist United Front in Malaya, 1945–1948.* Singapore: Times Books, 1979.

Chen, King C. *Vietnam and China, 1938–1954.* Princeton: Princeton University Press, 1969.

Cheng, Lim-Keak. *Social Change and the Chinese in Singapore, Economic Geography with Special Reference to Bang Structure.* Singapore: Singapore University Press, 1985.

Chew, Ernest C. T., and Edwin Lee. *A History of Singapore.* Singapore: Oxford University Press, 1991.

Chia, Felix. *Ala Sayang: A Social History of the Chinese Babas.* Singapore: Times Publishers, 1983.

Chin, John M. *The Sarawak Chinese.* Kuala Lumpur: Oxford University Press, 1981.

Chirot, Daniel, and Anthony Reid. *Essential Outsiders: Chinese and Jews in the Modern Transformation of Southeast Asia and Central Europe.* Seattle: University of Washington Press, 1997.

Christie, Clive J. *Ideology and Revolution in Southeast Asia, 1900–1975: Political Ideas of the Anti-Colonial Era.* Richmond: Curzon Press, 2000.

Chua, Beng Huat. *Communitarian Ideology and Democracy in Singapore.* London: Routledge, 1995.

Chua, Beng Huat. *Liberalism Disavowed: Communitarianism and State Capitalism in Singapore.* Singapore: NUS Press, 2017.

Clammer, John R. *Straits Chinese Society: Studies in the Sociology of Baba Communities in Malaysia and Singapore.* Singapore: Singapore University Press, 1980.

Clammer, John R. *The Sociology of Singapore Religion: Studies in Christianity and Chinese Culture*. Singapore: Chopmen Publishers, 1991.

Clark, Hugh R. *The Sinitic Encounter in Southeast China through the First Millennium*. Honolulu: University of Hawaii, 2016.

Coedes, George. *Les etats hindouises d'Indochine et d'Indonesie*. Paris: E. De Boccard, 1948.

Cohn, Bernard. *An Anthropologist Among the Historians and Other Essays*. New Delhi: Oxford University Press, 1987.

Cooper, Frederick, and Laura Ann Stoler. *Tensions of Empire: Colonial Cultures in a Bourgeois World*. Berkeley: University of California Press, 1997.

Corpuz, O. D. *The Roots of the Filipino Nation — Vol. 1 and Vol. 2*. Quezon City: Aklahi Foundation, 1989.

Craig, Albert M. *Civilization and Enlightenment: The Early Thought of Fukuzawa Yukichi*. Cambridge: Harvard University Press, 2009.

Curtin, Phillip D. *Cross-Cultural Trade in World History*. New York: Cambridge University Press, 1984.

Cushman, Jennifer, and Wang Gungwu. *Changing Identities of the Southeast Asian Chinese After World War II*. Hong Kong: Hong Kong University Press, 1988.

Darmaputera, Eka. *Pancasila and the Search for Identity and Modernity in Indonesian Society: A Cultural and Ethical Analysis*. Leiden: Brill, 1988.

Daus, Ronald. *Portuguese Eurasian Communities in Southeast Asia*. Singapore: Institute of Southeast Asian Studies, 1989.

De Bary, William Theodore. *East Asian Civilizations: A Dialogue in Five Stages*. Cambridge: Harvard University Press, 1988.

De la Costa, Horacio. *The Jesuits in the Philippines, 1581–1768*. Cambridge: Harvard University Press, 1961.

De Silva, Kinglsey M., Pensri Duke, Ellen S. Goldberg, and Nathan Katz. *Ethnic Conflict in Buddhist Societies: Sri Lanka, Thailand and Burma*. Boulder: Westview Press, 1998.

Diamond, Jared. *Guns, Germs, and Steel: The Fates of Human Societies*. New York: W. W. Norton & Co., 1997.

Diamond, Jared. *Upheaval: Turning Points for Nations in Crisis*. New York: Little, Brown and Company, 2019.

Dijk, Kees van. *Rebellion Under the Banner of Islam: The Darul Islam in Indonesia*. The Hague: Martinus Nijhoff, 1981.

Dijk, Kees van, and Nico J. G. Kaptein. *Islam, Politics and Change: The Indonesian Experience After the Fall of Suharto*. Leiden: Leiden University Press, 2016.

Dittmer, Lowell, and Samuel Kim. *China's Quest for National Identity*. Ithaca: Cornell University Press, 1993.

DuBois, Thomas David. *Casting Faiths: Imperialism and the Transformation of Religion in East and Southeast Asia*. London: Palgrave Macmillan, 2009.

Duignan, Peter, and L. H. Gann. *The Rebirth of the West: The Americanization of the Democratic World, 1945-1958*. Cambridge: Blackwell, 1992.

Duiker, William J. *The Rise of Nationalism in Vietnam, 1900-1941*. Ithaca: Cornell University Press, 1976.

Egger, Vernon O. *A History of the Muslim World to 1750: The Making of a Civilization*. 2nd ed. Oxon: Routledge, 2017.

Eisenstadt, S. N. *Comparative Civilizations and Multiple Modernities*. Leiden: Brill, 2003.

Eisenstadt, S. N. *Japanese Civilization: A Comparative View*. Chicago: University of Chicago Press, 1996.

Eisenstadt, S. N. *The Origins and Diversity of Axial Age Civilizations*. Albany: State University of New York Press, 1986.

Eliraz, Giora. *Islam in Indonesia: Modernism, Radicalism and the Middle East Dimension*. Brighton: Sussex Academic Press, 2004.

Elliott, John H. *The Hispanic World: Civilization and Empire, Europe and the Americas, Past and Present*. London: Thames & Hudson, 1992.

Enloe, Cynthia H. Multi-Ethnic Politics: *The Case of Malaysia*. Berkeley: University of California Press, 1970.

Esposito, John L. *Islam in Asia: Religion, Politics and Society*. New York: Oxford University Press, 1987.

Fairbank, John K. *The Chinese World Order: Traditional China's Foreign Relations*. Cambridge: Harvard University Press, 1968.

Fairbank, John K., and Edwin O. Reischauer. *China: Tradition & Transformation*. Boston: Houghton Mifflin, 1978.

Farish Noor. *From Majapahit to Putrajaya: Searching for Another Malaysia*. Kuala Lumpur: Silverfish Books, 2005.

Faure, David, and Tao Tao Liu. *Unity and Diversity: Local Cultures and Identities in China*. Hong Kong: Hong Kong University Press, 1996.
Fealy, Greg, and Virginia Hooker. *Voices of Islam in Southeast Asia: A Contemporary Sourcebook*. Singapore: Institute of Southeast Asian Studies, 2006.
Feith, Herbert. *The Decline of Constitutional Democracy in Indonesia*. Ithaca: Cornell University Press, 1962.
Feith, Herbert, and Lance Castles. *Indonesian Political Thinking, 1945–1965*. Ithaca: Cornell University Press, 1970.
Ferguson, Niall. *Civilisation: The West and the Rest*. London: Allen Lane, 2011.
Ferguson, Niall. *Colossus: The Price of America's Empire*. New York: Penguin Press, 2004.
Feuerstein, Georg, Subhash Kak, and David Frawley. *The Search of the Cradle of Civilization: New Light on Ancient India*. Wheaton: Quest Books, 1995.
Fitzgerald, Charles Patrick. *The Southern Expansion of the Chinese People: Southern Fields and Southern Ocean*. London: Barrie & Jenkins, 1972.
Fitzgerald, John. *Awakening China: Politics, Culture, and Class in the Nationalist Revolution*. Stanford: Stanford University Press, 1996.
Fitzgerald, John. *Cadre Country: How China Became the Chinese Communist Party*. Sydney: University of New South Wales Press, 2022.
Fitzgerald, Stephen. *China and the Overseas Chinese: A study of Peking's Changing Policy, 1949–1970*. Cambridge: Cambridge University Press, 1972.
Fogel, Joshua A., and Peter G. Zarrow. *Imagining the People: Chinese Intellectuals and the Concept of Citizenship, 1890–1920*. New York: M. E. Sharpe, 1997.
Fox, Jim, and Clifford Sather. *Origins, Ancestry, and Alliance: Explorations in Austronesian Ethnography*. Canberra: Australian National University Research School of Asia and Pacific Studies, 1996.
Frank, Andre Gunder. *Reorient: Global Economy in an Asian Age*. Berkeley: University of California Press, 1998.
Freedman, Maurice. *Chinese Family and Marriage in Singapore*. London: Her Majesty's Stationery Office, 1957.
Freedman, Maurice. *The Study of Chinese Society*. Stanford: Stanford University Press, 1979.
Funston, John. *Malay Politics: A Study of UMNO and PAS*. Kuala Lumpur: Heinemann, 1980.

Furnivall, J. S. *Colonial Policy and Practice: A Comparative Study of Burma and Netherlands India.* Cambridge: Cambridge University Press, 1948.

Gagliano, F. V. *Communal Violence in Malaysia, 1969: The Political Aftermath.* Athens: Ohio University Press, 1970.

Gehrke, Hans-Joachim. *Making Civilizations: The World Before 600.* Cambridge: The Belknap Press of Harvard University Press, 2020.

Giersch, C. Patterson. *Asian Borderlands: The Transformation of Qing China's Yunnan Frontier.* Cambridge: Harvard University Press, 2006.

Goscha, Christopher E. *Vietnam or Indochina: Contesting Concepts of Space, 1887–1954.* Copenhagen: Nordic Institute of Asian Studies, 1995.

Griffiths, Arlo, Andrew Hardy, and Geoff Wade. *Champa: Territories and Networks of a Southeast Asian Kingdom.* Paris: Ecole francaise d'Extreme-Orient, 2019.

Groslier, Bernard Philippe. *Angkor: Art and Civilization.* London: Thames and Hudson, 1957.

Gullick, J. M. *Malaya.* London: E. Benn, 1963.

Guy, John. *Lost Kingdoms: Hindu–Buddhist Sculpture of Early Southeast Asia.* New York: The Metropolitan Museum of Art; New Haven: Yale University Press, 2014.

Hagerman, C. A. *Britain's Imperial Muse: The Classics, Imperialism, and the Indian Empire, 1784–1914.* London: Palgrave Macmillan, 2013.

Hall, D. G. E. *A History of South-East Asia.* 3rd ed. London: Macmillan, 1977.

Hall, Kenneth R. *Maritime Trade and State Development in Early Southeast Asia.* Honolulu: University of Hawaii Press, 1984.

Hamashita, Takeshi. *China, East Asia and the Global Economy: Regional and Historical Perspectives.* Edited by Linda Grove and Mark Selden. Oxon: Routledge, 2008.

Hamilton, Gary G. *Cosmopolitan Capitalists: Hong Kong and the Chinese Diaspora at the End of the 29th Century.* Seattle: University of Washington Press, 1999.

Hang, Xing. *Conflict and Commerce in Maritime East Asia: The Zheng Family and the Shaping of the Modern World, 1620–1720.* Cambridge: Cambridge University Press, 2016.

Hara, Fujio. *Malayan Chinese and China: Conversion in Identity Consciousness, 1945–1957.* Tokyo: Institute of Developing Economies, 1997.

Harrell, Stevan. *Cultural Encounters on China's Ethnic Frontiers.* Seattle: University of Washington Press, 1995.

Harrison, Tom. *The Malays of Southwest Sarawak Before Malaysia*. London: Macmillan, 1970.

Harvey, David Allen. *The French Enlightenment and its Others: The Mandarin, the Savage, and the Invention of the Human Sciences*. New York: Palgrave Macmillan, 2012.

Hassan, Riaz. *Singapore Society in Transition*. Kuala Lumpur: Oxford University Press, 1976.

Headley, John M. *The Europeanization of the World: On the Origins of Human Rights and Democracy*. Princeton: Princeton University Press, 2007.

Hefner, Robert W. *Civil Islam: Muslims and Democratization in Indonesia*. Princeton: Princeton University Press, 2000.

Hefner, Robert W. *Market Cultures: Society and Values in the New Asian Capitalisms*. Singapore: Institute of Southeast Asian Studies, 1998.

Heng, Derek. *Sino-Malay Trade and Diplomacy from the Tenth through the Fourteenth Century*. Athens: Ohio University Press, 2012.

Heng, Pek Koon. *Chinese Politics in Malaysia: A History of the Malayan Chinese Association*. Singapore: OUP, 1988.

Hewison, Kevin. *Power and Politics in Thailand*. Manila: Contemporary Asia Publishers, 1989.

Hickey, Gerald C. *Sons of the Mountains: Ethnohistory of the Vietnamese Central Highlands to 1954*. New Haven: Yale University Press, 1983.

Higham, Charles. *The Civilization of Angkor*. London: Weidenfeld & Nicolson, 2001.

Hill, Ann Maxwell. *Merchants and Migrants: Ethnicity and Trade Among Yunnanese Chinese in Southeast Asia*. New Haven: Yale University Southeast Asia Studies, 1998.

Ho, Eng Seng. *The Graves of Tarim: Genealogy and Mobility Across the Indian Ocean*. Berkeley: University of California Press, 2006.

Hobsbawm, Eric. *The Age of Empire 1875–1915*. New York: Vintage Books, 1989.

Hobson, John M. *The Eastern Origins of Western Civilisation*. New York: Cambridge University Press, 2004.

Hong, Hai. *The Rule of Culture: Corporate and State Governance in China and East Asia*. New York: Routledge, 2020.

Hooker, Virginia, and Norani Othman. *Malaysia: Islam, Society and Politics*. Singapore: Institute of Southeast Asian Studies, 2003.

Howland, Douglas R. *Borders of Chinese Civilisation: Geography and History at Empire's End*. Durham: Duke University Press, 1996.

Hua, Wu Yin. *Class and Communalism in Malaysia: Politics in a Dependent Capitalist State*. London: Zed Press, 1983.

Huang, Philip C. *Liang Ch'i-ch'ao and Modern Chinese Liberalism*. Seattle: University of Washington Press, 1972.

Huntington, Samuel P. *The Clash of Civilizations and the Remaking of World Order*. New York: Simon & Schuster, 1996.

Husin Ali, Syed. *Ethnic Relations in Malaysia: Harmony & Conflict*. Petaling Jaya: Strategic Information and Research Development Centre, 2008.

Husin Ali, Syed. *Malay Peasant Society and Leadership*. Kuala Lumpur: Oxford University Press, 1975.

Ibrahim, Azhar. *Contemporary Islamic Discourse in the Malay-Indonesian World: Critical Perspectives*. Petaling Jaya: Strategic Information and Research Development Centre, 2014.

Ibrahim, Zawawi, Gareth Richards, and Victor T. King. *Discourses, Agency and Identity in Malaysia: Critical Perspectives*. Singapore: Springer, 2021.

Ivanova, Mariya I. *The Black Sea and the Early Civilizations of Europe, the Near East and Asia*. Cambridge: Cambridge University Press, 2013.

Jacq-Hergoualc'h, Michel. *The Malay Peninsula: Crossroads of the Maritime Silk Road (100 BC–1300 AD)*. Translated by Victoria Hobson. Leiden: Brill, 2002.

Jacques, Claude, and Philippe Lafond. *The Khmer Empire: Cities and Sanctuaries: Fifth to the Thirteenth Century*. Bangkok: River Books, 2007.

Jory, Patrick. *From "Melayu Patani" to "Thai Muslim": The Spectre of Ethnic Identity in Southern Thailand*. Singapore: Asia Research Institute, National University of Singapore, 2007.

Kahn, Joel S., and Francis Loh Kok Wah. *Fragmented Vision: Culture and Politics in Contemporary Malaysia*. Sydney: Allen and Unwin, 1992.

Kaldellis, Anthony. *Hellenism in Byzantium: The Transformations of Greek Identity and the Reception of the Classical Tradition*. Cambridge: Cambridge University Press, 2007.

Kassim, Ismail. *Problems of Elite Cohesion: A Perspective From a Minority Community*. Singapore: Singapore University Press, 1974.

Katzenstein, Peter J. *Civilizations in World Politics: Plural and Pluralist Perspectives.* London: Routledge, 2010.

Keddie, Nikki R. *Iran and the Muslim World: Resistance and Revolution.* London: Palgrave Macmillan, 1995.

Kenley, David L. *New Culture in a New World: The May Fourth Movement and the Chinese Diaspora in Singapore.* New York: Routledge, 2003.

Kennedy, Paul M. *The Parliament of Man: The Past, Present, and Future of the United Nations.* New York: Random House, 2006.

Kennedy, Paul M. *The Rise and Fall of the Great Powers: Economic Change and Military Conflict from 1500 to 2000.* New York: Random House, 1987.

Kerkvliet, Benedict J. Tria. *Everyday Politics in the Philippines: Class and Status Relations in a Central Luzon Village.* Berkeley: University of California Press, 1990.

Kessler, Clive S. *Islam and Politics in a Malay State: Kelantan 1938–1969.* Ithaca: Cornell UP, 1978.

Keyes, Charles F. *Thailand: Buddhist Kingdom as Modern Nation-State.* Boulder: Westview Press, 1989.

Keyes, Charles F., Laurel Kendall, and Helen Hardacre. *Asian Visions of Authority: Religion and the Modern States of East and Southeast Asia.* Honolulu: University of Hawaii Press, 1994.

Khairudin Aljunied, Syed Muhd. *Colonialism, Violence and Muslims in Southeast Asia: The Maria Hertogh Controversy and its Aftermath.* New York: Routledge, 2009.

Khairudin Aljunied, Syed Muhd. *Muslim Cosmopolitanism: Southeast Asian Islam in Comparative Perspective.* Edinburgh: Edinburgh University Press, 2017.

Khoo, Boo Teik. *Paradoxes of Mahathirism: An Intellectual Biography of Mahathir Mohamad.* Kuala Lumpur: Oxford University Press, 1995.

Khoo, Joo Ee. *The Straits Chinese: A Cultural History.* Amsterdam: The Pepin Press, 1996.

Kotkin, Joel. *Tribes: How Race, Religion, and Identity Determine Success in the New Global Economy.* New York: Random House, 1992.

Kroeber, A. L. *The Nature of Culture.* Chicago: University of Chicago Press, 1952.

Kuhn, Philip A. *Chinese Among Others: Emigration in Modern Times.* Singapore: NUS Press, 2008.

Kulke, Hermann, K. Kesavapany, and Vijay Sakhuja. *Nagapattinam to Suvarnadwipa: Reflections on the Chola Naval Expeditions to Southeast Asia.* Singapore: Institute of Southeast Asan Studies, 2009.

Kunstadter, Peter. *Southeast Asian Tribes, Minorities, and Nations — Vol. 1 and Vol. 2.* Princeton: Princeton University Press, 1967.

Kwa, Chong-Guan. *Early Southeast Asia Viewed from India: An Anthology of Articles from the Greater India Society.* New Delhi: Manohar Publishers, 2013.

Laffan, Michael F. *Islamic Nationhood and Colonial Indonesia: The Umma Below the Winds.* London: Routledge, 2003.

Lai, Ah Eng. *Meanings of Multiethnicity: A Case-Study of Ethnicity and Ethnic Relations in Singapore.* Kuala Lumpur: Oxford University Press, 1995.

Lal, V. Brij, Peter Reeves, and Rajesh Rai. *The Encyclopedia of the Indian Diaspora.* Singapore: Didier Millet in Association with the National University of Singapore, 2002.

Lammerts, D. Christian. *Buddhist Dynamics in Premodern and Early Modern Southeast Asia.* Singapore: Institute of Southeast Asian Studies, 2015.

Lapian, Adrian B. *Orang Laut, Bajak Laut, Raja Laut: Sejarah Kawasan Laut Sulawesi abad XIX.* Depok: Komunitas Bambu, 2011.

Lee, Christopher J. *Making a World After Empire: The Bandung Moment and its Political Afterlives.* Athens, OH: Ohio University Press, 2010.

Lee, Kuan Yew. *From Third World to First: The Singapore Story, 1965–2000.* Singapore: Times Editions, 2000.

Lee, Kuan Yew. *The Singapore Story: Memoirs of Lee Kuan Yew.* Singapore: Times Editions, 1998.

Lee, Ting Hui. *The Communist Organisation in Singapore: Its Techniques of Manpower Mobilisation and Management, 1948–1966.* Singapore: Institute of Southeast Asian Studies, 1976.

Leigh, Michael. *The Rising Moon: Political Change in Sarawak.* Sydney: Sydney University Press, 1974.

Leow, Rachel. *Taming Babel: Language in the Making of Malaysia.* Cambridge: Cambridge University Press, 2018.

Li, Xueqin. *Eastern Zhou and Qin Civilizations.* Translated by K. C. Chang. New Haven: Yale University Press, 1985.

Lieberman, Victor. *Strange Parallels: Southeast Asia in Global Context, 800–1830, Vol. 1: Integration on the Mainland*. Cambridge: Cambridge University Press, 2003.

Lim, Linda Y. C., and Peter Gosling. *The Chinese in Southeast Asia — Vol 1. and Vol. 2*. Singapore: Maruzen Asia, 1983.

Lim, Teck Ghee. *Origins of a Colonial Economy: Land and Agriculture in Perak 1874–1897*. Penang: Penerbit Universiti Sains Malaysia, 1976.

Linklater, Andrew. *Violence and Civilization in the Western States-Systems*. Cambridge: Cambridge University Press, 2016.

Liow, Joseph Chinyong. *Islam, Education and Reform in Southern Thailand: Tradition and Transformation*. Singapore: Institute of Southeast Asian Studies, 2009.

Lipset, Seymour. M. *The First New Nation: The United States in Historical and Comparative Perspective*. London: Heinemann, 1964.

Lomperis, Timothy J. *From People's War to People's Rule: Insurgency, Intervention, and the Lessons of Vietnam*. Chapel Hill: University of North Carolina Press, 1996.

Mackie, J. A. C. *Konfrontasi: The Indonesia–Malaysia Dispute, 1963–1966*. Kuala Lumpur: Oxford University Press, 1974.

Maddison, Angus. *The World Economy: Vol. 1: A Millennial Perspective; and Vol. 2: Historical Statistics*. Paris: OECD Publishing, 2006.

Mahizhnan, Arun, and Nalina Gopal. *Sojourners to Settlers: Tamils in Singapore — Vol. 1 and Vol. 2*. Singapore: Indian Heritage Centre and Institute of Policy Studies, 2019.

Maideen, Haja. *The Nadra Tragedy: The Maria Hertogh Controversy*. Petaling Jaya: Pelanduk Publications, 1989.

Majul, Cesar. *Muslims in the Philippines*. Quezon City: University of the Philippines Press, 1973.

Mak, Lau Fong. *The Sociology of Secret Societies: A Study of Chinese Secret Societies in Singapore and Peninsular Malaysia*. Kuala Lumpur: Oxford University Press, 1981.

Manguin, Pierre-Yves, A. Mani, and Geoff Wade. *Early Interactions between South and Southeast Asia: Reflections on Cross-Cultural Exchanges*. Singapore: Institute of Southeast Asian Studies, 2011.

Manickam, Sandra Khor. *Taming the Wild: Aborigines and Racial Knowledge in Colonial Malaya*. Singapore: NUS Press, 2015.

Mann, Susan. *Local Merchants and the Chinese Bureaucracy, 1750–1950*. Stanford: Stanford University Press, 1987.

Marr, David G. *Vietnamese Anticolonialism: 1885–1925*. Berkeley: University of California, 1971.

Mazlish, Bruce. *Civilization and its Contents*. Stanford: Stanford University Press, 2004.

McCargo, Duncan. *Tearing Apart the Land: Islam and Legitimacy in Southern Thailand*. Ithaca: Cornell University Press, 2008.

McPherson, Kenneth. *The Indian Ocean: A History of People and the Sea*. Delhi: Oxford University Press, 1993.

Meddeb, Abdelwahab. *Islam and the Challenge of Civilization*. Translated by Jane Kuntz. New York: Fordham University Press, 2013.

Mehden, Fred R. von der. *Religion and Nationalism in Southeast Asia*. Wisconsin: University of Wisconsin Press, 1963.

Mehden, Fred R. von der. *Two Worlds of Islam: Interaction Between Southeast Asia and the Middle East*. Gainsville: University of Florida Press, 1993.

Milner, Anthony. *The Invention of Politics in Colonial Malaya: Contesting Nationalism and the Expansion of the Public Sphere*. Cambridge: Cambridge University Press, 1994.

Mintz, Jeanne S. *Mohammed, Marx and Marhaen: The Roots of Indonesian Socialism*. London: Pall Mall Press, 1965.

Moedjanto, G. *The Concept of Power in Javanese Culture*. Yogyakarta: Gadjah Mada University Press, 1986.

Mohamad, Mahathir. *The Malay Dilemma*. Kuala Lumpur: Federal Publications, 1970.

Mu, Chi'en. *Traditional Government in Imperial China: A Critical Analysis*. Translated by Chun-tu Hsueh and George O. Totten. Hong Kong: Chinese University Press, 1982.

Muljono, Slamet. *Menudju Puntjak Kemegahan: Sedjarah Keradjaan Madjapahit*. Jakarta: Balai Pustaka, 1965.

Munoz, Paul Michel. *Early Kingdoms of the Indonesian Archipelago and the Malay Peninsula*. Paris: Editions Didier Millet, 2006.

Mutalib, Hussin. *Singapore Malays: Being Ethnic Minority and Muslim in a Global City*. London: Routledge, 2012.

Muzaffar, Chandra. *Islamic Resurgence in Malaysia*. Petaling Jaya: Fajar Bakti, 1987.

Nagata, Judith. A. *Malaysian Mosaic: Perspectives From a Poly-Ethnic Society*. Vancouver: University of British Columbia Press, 1979.

Nagata, Judith. A. *The Reflowering of Islam in Malaysia: Modern Religious Radicals and Their Roots*. Vancouver: UBC Press, 1984.

Nakamura, Matsuo. *The Crescent Arises Over the Banyan Tree: A Study of the Muhammadiyah Movement in a Central Javanese Town, c.1910s–2010. Second Enlarged Edition*. Singapore: Institute of Southeast Asian Studies, 2012.

Nash, Manning. *Peasant Citizens: Politics, Religion and Modernization in Kelantan, Malaysia*. Athens: Ohio University Center for International Studies, 1974.

Ngaosrivathana, Mayoury, and Kennon Breazeale. *Breaking New Ground in Lao History: Essays on the Seventh to Twentieth Centuries*. Chiang Mai: Silkworm Books, 2002.

Nieuwenhuijze, C. A. O. van. *Aspects of Islam in Post-Colonial Indonesia: Five Essays*. The Hague: Van Hoeve, 1958.

Nishizaki, Yoshinori. *Dynastic Democracy: Political Families in Thailand*. Madison, WI: The University of Wisconsin Press, 2022.

Nyce, Ray. *Chinese New Village in Malaysia: A Community Study*. Singapore: Malaysian Sociological Research Institute, 1973.

Nyíri, Pal, and Joana Breidenbach. *China Inside Out: Contemporary Chinese Nationalism and Transnationalism*. New York: Central European University Press, 2005.

Omar, Ariffin. *Bangsa Melayu: Malay Concepts of Democracy and Community, 1945–1950*. Kuala Lumpur: Oxford University Press, 1993.

Omohundro, John T. *Chinese Merchant Families in Iloilo: Commerce and Kin in a Central Philippine City*. Quezon City: Ateneo de Manila University Press, 1981.

Ong, Aihwa. *Flexible Citizenship: The Cultural Logics of Transnationality*. Durham: Duke University Press, 2000.

Ongkili, James P. *Nation-Building in Malaysia, 1946–1974*. Kuala Lumpur: Oxford University Press, 1985.

Ooi, Kee Beng. *The Eurasian Core and its Edges: Dialogues with Wang Gungwu on the History of the World*. Singapore: Institute of Southeast Asian Studies, 2015.

O'Reilly, Dougald J. W. *Early Civilizations of Southeast Asia*. Lanham: AltaMira Press, 2006.

Osborne, Milton. *The Mekong: Turbulent Past, Uncertain Future*. New York: Atlantic Monthly Press, 2000.
Pan, Lynn. *Sons of the Yellow Emperor*. London: Secker & Warburg, 1990.
Pan, Lynn. *The Encyclopedia of Chinese Overseas*. Richmond, Surrey: Curzon, 1999.
Park, Hyunhee. *Mapping the Chinese and Islamic Worlds: Cross-Cultural Exchanges in Pre-Modern Asia*. Cambridge: Cambridge University Press, 2012.
Pathmanathan, Murugasu, and R. Haas. *Political Culture: The Challenge of Modernisation*. Petaling Jaya: Centre for Policy Sciences, 1995.
Pearson, Michael. *Trade, Circulation, and Flow in the Indian Ocean*. Houndsmills, UK: Palgrave Macmillan, 2015.
Pigeaud, Theodore G. Th. *Java in the 14th Century: A Study in Cultural History: The Nāgara-Kĕrtāgama by Rakawi Prapañca of Majapahit, 1365 A.D.* The Hague: Martinus Nijhoff, 1960–1963.
Pillai, Gopinath, and K. Kesavapany. *50 years of Indian Community in Singapore*. Singapore: World Scientific, 2016.
Pineo, Ly-Tio-Fane. *Chinese Diaspora in Western Indian Ocean*. Mauritius: Editions de l'Ocean Indien and Chinese Catholic Mission, 1985.
Pitsuwan, Surin. *Islam and Malay Nationalism: A Case Study of the Malay-Muslims of Southern Thailand*. Bangkok: Thammasat University Thai Khadi Research Institute, 1985.
Platzdasch, Bernard, and Johan Saravanamuttu. *Religious Diversity in Muslim Majority States in Southeast Asia: Areas of Toleration and Conflict*. Singapore: Institute of Southeast Asian Studies, 2014.
Pomeranz, Kenneth. *The Great Divergence: China, Europe, and the Making of the Modern World*. Princeton: Princeton University Press, 2000.
Prakash, Om. *The Trading World of the Indian Ocean, 1500–1800*. New Delhi: Centre for Studies in Civilisations: Pearson, 2012.
Ptak, Roderich. *China's Seaborne Trade with South and Southeast Asia, 1200–1750*. Vermont: Ashgate Publishing Company, 1998.
Ptak, Roderich, and Dietmar Rothermund. *Emporia, Commodities and Entrepreneurs in Asian Maritime Trade, c. 1400–1750*. Stuttgart: Franz Steiner, 1991.
Purcell, Victor. *The Chinese in Southeast Asia*. 2nd ed. Kuala Lumpur: Oxford University Press, 1980.

Purushotam, Nirmala. *Negotiating Multiculturalism: Disciplining Difference in Singapore*. Berlin: De Gruyter, 2000.

Pye, Lucian W. *Guerilla Communism in Malaya: Its Social and Political Meaning*. Princeton: Princeton University Press, 1956.

Pye, Lucian W. *Politics, Personality and Nation Building: Burma's Search for Identity*. New Haven: Yale University Press, 1962.

Rahim, Lily Zubaidah. *Singapore in the Malay World: Building and Breaching Regional Bridges*. Abingdon, Oxon: Routledge, 2009.

Ratnam, K. J. *Communalism and the Political Process in Malaya*. Kuala Lumpur: University of Malaya Press, 1965.

Reid, Anthony. *Sojourners and Settlers: Histories of Southeast Asia and the Chinese*. Sydney: Allen & Unwin, 1993.

Reid, Anthony. *Southeast Asia in the Age of Commerce, 1450–1680, Vol. 1: The Lands Below the Winds*. New Haven: Yale University Press, 1988.

Reid, Anthony. *Southeast Asia in the Age of Commerce, 1450–1680, Vol. 2: Expansion and Crisis*. New Haven: Yale University Press, 1993.

Reynolds, Craig J. *Thai Radical Discourse: The Real Face of Thai Feudalism Today*. Ithaca: Cornell University Press, 2018.

Ricklefs, Merle C. *A History of Modern Indonesia: c. 1300 to the Present*. London: Macmillan, 1981.

Roff, William R. *The Origins of Malay Nationalism*. Kuala Lumpur: University of Malaya Press, 1967.

Said, Edward. *Orientalism*. New York: Vintage Books, 1994.

Salmon, Claudine, and Lombard Denys. *Les Chinois de Jakarta: Temples et vie Collective*. Paris: SECMI, 1977.

Sandhu, Kernial Singh. *Indians in Malaya: Immigration and Settlement, 1786–1957*. Cambridge: Cambridge University Press, 1969.

Sandhu, Kernial Singh, and A. Mani. *Indian Communities in Southeast Asia*. Singapore: Times Academic Press, 1995.

Sandin, Benedict. *The Sea Dayaks of Borneo Before White Rajah Rule*. London: Macmillan, 1968.

Sastri, Nilakanta. *South Indian Influences in the Far East*. Bombay: Hind Kitabs, 1949.

Schottenhammer, Angela. *The East Asian "Mediterranean": Maritime Crossroads of Culture, Commerce, and Human Migration.* Wiesbaden: Harrassowitz Verlag, 2008.

Schwarcz, Vera. *The Chinese Enlightenment: Intellectuals and the Legacy of the May Fourth Movement.* Berkeley: University of California Press, 1986.

Schwartz, Benjamin I. *The World of Thought in Ancient China.* Cambridge: Belknap Press of Harvard University Press, 1985.

Scott, William Henry. *The Discovery of the Igorots: Spanish Contacts with the Pagans of Northern Luzon.* Quezon City: New Day Publishers, 1974.

See, Teresita Ang. *Ethnic Chinese in the Philippines.* Manila: Kaisa Para Sa Kaunlaran, 1996.

Shamsul, A. B. *From British to Bumiputera Rule: Local Politics and Rural Development in Peninsular Malaysia.* Singapore: Institute of Southeast Asian. Studies, 1986.

Siddique, Sharon, and Nirmala Purushotam. *Singapore's Little India: Past, Present and Future.* Singapore: Institute of Southeast Asian. Studies, 1982.

Sikri, Veena. *India and Malaysia: Intertwined Strands.* Singapore: Institute of Southeast Asian Studies, 2013.

Silverstein, Josef. *Burmese Politics: The Dilemma of National Unity.* New Brunswick: Rutgers University Press, 1980.

Singer, Milton. *When a Great Tradition Modernizes: An Anthropological Approach to Indian Civilization.* London: Pall Mall Press, 1972.

Skinner, G. William. *Chinese Society in Thailand: An Analytical History.* Ithaca: Cornell University Press, 1957.

Smail, John R. W. *Bandung in the Early Revolution, 1945–1946: A Study in the Social History of the Indonesian Revolution.* Ithaca: Cornell Southeast Asia Program, 1964.

Smith, Anthony D. *The Ethnic Origins of Nations.* Oxford: Blackwell, 1986.

Smith, Jeremy C. A. *Debating Civilisations: Interrogating Civilisational Analysis in a Global Age.* Manchester: Manchester University Press, 2017.

Smith, Martin. *Burma: Insurgency and the Politics of Ethnicity.* London: Zed Press, 1999.

Snellgrove, David. *Angkor — Before and After: A Cultural History of the Khmers.* Bangkok: Orchid Press, 2004.

So, Billy K. L., John Fitzgerald, Huang Jianli, and James K. Chin. *Power and Identity in the Chinese World Order: Festschrift in Honour of Professor Wang Gungwu*. Hong Kong: Hong Kong University Press, 2003.

Soemardjan, Selo. *Social Change in Jogjakarta*. Ithaca: Cornell University Press, 1962.

Sopiee, Mohamed Noordin. *From Malayan Union to Singapore Separation: Political Unification in the Malaysian Union, 1945–1965*. Kuala Lumpur: University of Malaya Press, 1974.

Souza, George B. *The Survival of Empire: Portuguese Trade and Society in China and the South China Sea, 1630–1754*. Cambridge: Cambridge University Press, 1986.

Sowell, Thomas. *The Economics and Politics of Race: An International Perspective*. New York: Quill, 1983.

Steinberg, David I. *Burma: A Socialist Nation of Southeast Asia*. Boulder: Westview Press, 1982.

Steinberg, David Joel. *In Search of Southeast Asia: A Modern History*. Kuala Lumpur: Oxford University Press, 1971.

Steinberg, David Joel. *The Philippines: A Singular and a Plural Place*. 3rd ed. Boulder: Westview Press, 1990.

Strauch, Judith. *Chinese Politics in the Malaysian State*. Cambridge: Harvard University Press, 1981.

Stuart-Fox, Martin. *A History of Laos*. Cambridge: Cambridge University Press, 1997.

Stuurman, Siep. *The Invention of Humanity: Equality and Cultural Difference in World History*. Cambridge: Harvard University Press, 2017.

Subrahmanyam, Sanjay. *Europe's India: Words, People, Empires, 1500–1800*. Cambridge: Harvard University Press, 2017.

Sukarno. *Nationalism, Islam, and Marxism*. Translated by Karel H. Warouw and Peter D. Weldon, with an introduction by Ruth T. McVey. Ithaca: Cornell Southeast Asia Program, 1970.

Sundaram, Jomo K. *A Question of Class: Capital, The State and Uneven Development in Malaya*. New York: Monthly Review Press, 1988.

Suryadinata, Leo. *Ethnic Chinese in Singapore and Malaysia: A Dialogue Between Tradition and Modernity*. Singapore: Times Academic Press, 2002.

Suryadinata, Leo. *Pribumi Indonesians, the Chinese Minority and China*. Singapore: Heinemann, 1992.

Suzuki, Shogo. *Civilisation and Empire: China and Japan's Encounter with European International Society*. New York: Routledge, 2009.

Tagliacozzo, Eric. *In Asian Waters: Oceanic Worlds From Yemen to Yokohama*. Princeton: Princeton University Press, 2022.

Tamney, Joseph B. *The Struggle Over Singapore's Soul: Western Modernization and Asian Culture*. Berlin: Walter de Gruyter, 1996.

Tan, Antonio S. *The Chinese in the Philippines, 1898–1935: A Study of Their National Awakening*. Quezon City: R. P. Garcia, 1972.

Tan, Chee Beng. *Chinese Peranakan Heritage in Malaysia and Singapore*. Kuala Lumpur: Penerbit Fajar Bakti, 1991.

Tan, Chung, and Geng Yinzeng. *India and China: Twenty Centuries of Civilization Interaction and Vibrations*. New Delhi: History of Indian Science, Philosophy and Culture Project, Centre for Studies in Civilizations, 2005.

Tan, Giok-Lan. *The Chinese of Sukabumi: A Study in Social and Cultural Accommodation*. Ithaca: Southeast Asia Program, Cornell University, 1963.

Tan, Liok Ee. *The Rhetoric of Bangsa and Minzu: Community and Nation in Tension, the Malay Peninsula, 1951–1987*. Melbourne: Monash University Centre of Southeast Asian Studies, 1988.

Taylor, Keith Weller. *The Birth of Vietnam*. Berkeley: University of California Press, 1983.

Taylor, Robert H. *The State of Burma*. London: Hurst, 1987.

Teeuw, A., and David K. Wyatt. *Hikayat Patani — The Story of Patani*. The Hague: Martinus Nijhoff, 1970.

Tham, Seong Chee. *Malays and Modernisation: A Sociological Interpretation*. Singapore: Singapore University Press, 1977; 1983.

Tibi, Bassam. *Islam in Global Politics: Conflict and Cross-Civilizational Bridging*. London: Routledge, 2012.

Tinker, Hugh. *The Union of Burma*. London: Oxford University Press, 1967.

Tonnesson, Stein, and Hans Antlov. *Asian Forms of the Nation*. London: Curzon Press, 1996.

Tonnesson, Stein, and Hans Antlov. *Imperial Policy and Southeast Asian Nationalism, 1930–1957*. London: Curzon Press, 1995.

Topin, Benedict. *Kadazandusun Our Sacred Identity: Our Sacred Divine-Human Identity, Heritage Worldviews, Beliefs, Culture, Justice, Spirituality, and Ecological*

Being. Kota Kinabalu: Kadazan Dusun Cultural Association, Socio-Cultural Heritage Division, 2017.

Tracy, James D. *The Political Economy of Merchant Empires: State Power and World Trade, 1350–1750*. Cambridge: Cambridge University Press, 1991.

Tracy, James D. *The Rise of Merchant Empires: Long-Distance Trade in the Early Modern World*. Cambridge: Cambridge University Press, 1990.

Tran, Ky Phuong, and Bruce M. Lockhart. *The Cham of Vietnam: History, Society and Art*. Singapore: NUS Press, 2011.

Tran, Thi Anh-Dao. *Rethinking Asian Capitalism: The Achievements and Challenges of Vietnam under Doi Moi*. Cham: Palgrave Macmillan, 2022.

Tu, Wei-ming. *Confucian Traditions in East Asian Modernity: Moral Education and Economic Culture in Japan and the Four Mini-Dragons*. Cambridge: Harvard University Press, 1996.

Tu, Wei-ming. *The Living Tree: The Changing Meaning of Being Chinese Today*. Stanford: Stanford University Press, 1994.

Turnbull, Constance Mary. *A History of Singapore, 1819–1988*. Rev. ed. Singapore: Oxford University Press, 1977 [1989].

Van, Dang Nghiem. *Ethnic Minorities in Vietnam*. Hanoi: GIOI Publishers, 1993.

Vasil, Raj K. *Politics in a Plural Society: A Study of Non-Communal Political Parties in West Malaysia*. Kuala Lumpur: Oxford University Press, 1971.

Vickery, Michael. *Cambodia 1975–1982*. Sydney: Allen & Unwin, 1984.

Viraphol, Sarasin. *Tribute and Profit: Sino-Siamese Trade 1652–1853*. Cambridge: Harvard University Press, 1977.

Vorys, Karl von. *Democracy Without Consensus: Communalism and Political Stability in Malaysia*. Princeton: Princeton University Press, 1975.

Wain, Barry. *Malaysian Maverick: Mahathir Mohamad in Turbulent Times*. New York: Palgrave Macmillan, 2009.

Wallerstein, Immanuel. *The Capitalist World-Economy*. Cambridge: Cambridge University Press, 1979.

Wang, Fei-Ling. *The China Order: Centralia, World Empire, and the Nature of Chinese Power*. Albany: State University of New York Press, 2017.

Wang, Gungwu. *Community and Nation: Essays on Southeast Asia and the Chinese*. Singapore: Heinneman, 1981.

Wang, Gungwu. *Malaysia: A Survey*. New York: Praeger, 1964.

Wang, Tai Peng. *The Origins of Chinese Kongsi*. Petaling Jaya: Pelanduk Publications, 1988.

Wertheim, W. F. *Indonesian Society in Transition*. The Hague: Van Hoeve, 1964.

Wheatley, Paul. *The Golden Khersonese: Studies in the Historical Geography of the Malay Peninsula Before A.D. 1500*. Kuala Lumpur: University of Malaya Press, 1961.

Wheatley, Paul. *Negara and Commandery: Origins of the Southeast Asian Urban Tradition*. Chicago: University of Chicago Press, 1983.

Wickberg, Edgar. *The Chinese in Philippine Life 1850–1898*. New Haven: Yale University Press, 1965.

Wijeyewardene, Gehan. *Ethnic Groups Across National Boundaries in Mainland Southeast Asia*. Singapore: Institute of Southeast Asian Studies, 1990.

Winichakul, Thongchai. *Siam Mapped: A History of the Geo-Body of a Nation*. Honolulu: University of Hawaii Press, 1994.

Wolters, O. W. *Early Indonesian Commerce: A Study of the Origins of Śrīvijaya*. Ithaca: Cornell University Press, 1967.

Wolters, O. W. *History, Culture, and Region in Southeast Asian Perspectives*. Singapore: Institute of Southeast Asian Studies, 1982.

Wolters, O. W. *The Fall of Śrīvijaya in Malay History*. Ithaca: Cornell University Press, 1970.

Womack, Brantly. *China Among Equals: Asymmetric Foreign Relationships in Asia*. Singapore: World Scientific, 2010.

Wyatt, David K. *The Politics of Reform in Thailand: Education in the Reign of King Chulalongkorn*. New Haven: Yale University Press, 1969.

Yang, Bin. *Between Winds and Clouds: The Making of Yunnan (Second Century BCE to Twentieth Century CE)*. New York: Columbia University Press, 2009.

Yao, Alice. *The Ancient Highlands of Southwestern China: From the Bronze Age to the Han Empire*. New York: Oxford University Press, 2016.

Yen, Ching Hwang. *A Social History of the Chinese in Singapore and Malaya 1800–1911*. Singapore: Oxford University Press, 1986.

Yen, Ching Hwang. *The Overseas Chinese and the 1911 Revolution: With Special Reference to Singapore and Malaya*. Kuala Lumpur: Oxford University Press, 1976.

Yeoh, Brenda S. K., and Lily Kong. *Portraits of Places: History, Community, and Identity in Singapore*. Singapore: Times Editions, 1995.

Yong, Ching Fatt. *Chinese Leadership and Power in Colonial Singapore*. Singapore: Times Academic Press, 1991.

Yong, Mun Cheong. *Asian Traditions and Modernization: Perspectives from Singapore*. Singapore: Times Academic Press, 1992.

Yoshihara, Kunio. *The Rise of Ersatz Capitalism in Southeast Asia*. Singapore: Oxford University Press, 1988.

Yuan, Xingpei, Yan Wenming, Zhang Chuanxi, and Lou Yule. *The History of Chinese Civilisation*. English text edited by David R. Knechtges. Cambridge: Cambridge University Press, 2012.

Zakariya, Hafiz. *Islam, Culture and History in the Malay World*. Kuala Nerus, Terengganu: Universiti Malaysia Terengganu Press, 2022.

Zarrow, Peter. *Abolishing Boundaries: Global Utopias in the Formation of Modern Chinese Political Thought, 1880–1940*. Albany: State University of New York Press, 2021.

Zhao, Gang. *The Qing Opening to the Ocean: Chinese Maritime Policies, 1654–1757*. Honolulu: University of Hawaii Press, 2013.

Zheng, Yongnian. *Discovering Chinese Nationalism in China: Modernization, Identity, and International Relations*. Cambridge: Cambridge University Press, 1999.

Index

Abbasid caliphate, 53, 64
Abdul Rahman, Tunku, 137
Aceh, 99
Acehnese Empire, 60
adat, 99, 113
Afghanistan, 26, 140, 144
Africa, 7, 52, 53, 88, 90, 140, 154
Afro-Asian Solidarity
    Conference, 136
Age of Empires, 13, 105
Age of Enlightenment, 4, 58, 128
Alaska, 100
Alexander the Great, 53, 71
Allison, Graham, 108
"All under Heaven" (*tianxia*), 101,
    144, 166
Al-Raniri, Nuruddin, 46
ancient, x, xi, 3, 4, 6–9, 11, 12, 14–16,
    38, 44, 51, 58, 60, 62–66, 72, 74, 75,
    77, 81, 82, 87–92, 96, 97, 101,
    104–106, 111, 119–121, 132, 143,
    144, 164, 167, 168
ancient Indic civilisation, 146
Anderson, Benedict, 106
Angkor, 17, 33, 43, 47, 94
Anglo-Dutch Treaty, 36, 72, 89, 91
Annam, 91
Asia, 6, 7, 11, 12, 31, 37, 39, 44, 48,
    52, 53, 56, 58, 60, 63, 65, 67, 71, 88,
    91, 105, 120, 130, 131, 159, 167
Assam, 97
Association of Southeast Asian
    Nations (ASEAN), x, 74, 133,
    136–140, 146–149, 152, 159–161

Assyria, 52
Ataturk, Mustafa Kemal, 107
Atlantic Ocean, 31, 56, 63
Austro-Hungary, 88, 106
Ayutthaya, 44, 45, 59

Babylon, 52
Bandung Conference, 133, 134
Bangka, 36
Banten, 60
Bay of Bengal, 20, 59
Belt and Road Initiative, 74
Bengal, 91, 92, 97
Bolshevik Revolution, 108
Bombay, 91
Bonaparte, Napoleon, 68, 89,
    90, 107
Borneo, 28, 80, 137
Borobudur, 80
Borobudur, Prambanan, 22
Bose, Subhas Chandra, 93
Bourbon France, 67
Britain, 128, 129, 131, 136
British Empire, 7, 18, 36, 72, 95, 101,
    126
British Raj, 89, 92
Buddhism, 18, 22, 28, 34, 45, 66, 80,
    93, 94, 114, 115, 121, 122
    Mahayana Buddhism, 16
    Mahayana Buddhists, 167
    Theravada Buddhism, 96, 97
Bugis, 26, 29, 68, 99
Burma, 43, 59, 91, 97, 110, 114, 127,
    135, 152

Calcutta, 68, 72, 91, 97
Cambodia, 43, 46, 91, 96, 114, 135, 138, 139, 147
Cantonese, 12
capitalism, 3, 56, 62, 70, 76, 89, 91, 104, 105, 107, 108, 110, 121, 128, 142, 144, 147, 163
Catholic, 30, 48, 50, 55, 57, 63–65, 68, 82, 98
Central Asia, 16, 20, 26, 53, 62, 100, 101, 140, 153
Ceylon, 91, 94, 97
Champa, 19, 23
Charles I (English king), 67
China, x, xi, 4, 8, 11–13, 15, 18, 20–22, 26, 28, 43, 44, 49, 50, 58, 60, 61, 68, 73–75, 78, 82, 88, 92, 96–98, 100–105, 111, 115, 116, 118, 119, 121–123, 127, 130, 131, 137, 138, 142–144, 146, 148, 149, 151, 153–155, 160, 161, 163, 164, 166, 167
China's Buddhist "Western Heaven", 21, 98
Chinese Communist Party (CCP), 76, 123, 127, 130, 137, 142, 148
Christian, 4, 7, 12, 45, 47, 50–52, 55–58, 60, 61, 66, 75, 80, 86, 88, 100, 102, 116, 147, 154, 167
Christian European civilisation, 51, 121, 128, 132, 133, 146
Christian Mediterranean, 24
Cochin China, 91
Cold War, 7, 127, 130, 132, 136, 140, 142, 146, 148

colonisation/colonialism, x, 37, 70, 87, 99, 105, 110, 127–129, 137
communism, 131, 136, 139, 143, 153, 163
Confucianism, 15, 44, 64, 80, 122, 167
Congress of Vienna, 90
Constantinople, 30, 53
Cossack, 100
Counter-Reformation, 57
Cromwell, Oliver, 67
Crusades, 53, 54, 60, 100, 116
Cultural Revolution (China, 1966), 142

da Gama, Vasco, 47, 58
Deng Xiaoping, 131, 142, 143
Diponegoro (Javanese prince), 99
Dobby, E. H. G., 13
Dravidian, 16
Dutch, 36, 37, 60–63, 68, 70, 73, 80, 91, 99, 113, 126, 127
Dutch East India Company, 45, 47, 56, 57, 67, 68, 88

East Asia, 114, 128
English East India Company, 56, 88
Enlightenment, 25, 29, 30, 63, 66, 88, 97, 102, 104, 108, 111, 120, 121, 128–130, 132, 136, 144, 166, 167
  Enlightenment civilisation, x, 86, 89, 96, 99, 105, 107, 109, 110, 127, 130, 131, 140, 143, 147, 155
  Enlightenment Modern, 105, 120, 127, 129, 133, 135, 136, 142–144, 146, 154, 163

Eurasia, 36, 48, 52, 64, 100, 130, 131
Europe, 4, 6, 7, 11, 31, 38, 46, 50–52, 58, 59, 62–64, 66–68, 70, 88, 90, 98, 103, 106–108, 110, 120, 122, 128, 130, 132, 163
European Christian civilisation, 34
European Christian missionaries, 20, 92, 93, 101, 133

Fansuri, Hamzah, 46
Fascism, 108
Fa Xian, 21
Fort Canning Park, 25
France, 24, 37, 45, 67, 89, 91, 106, 107, 129, 131, 136
Fujian, 82, 116, 118
Fukuyama, Francis, 82, 140
Funan, 16
Furnivall, John Sydenham, 73

Gandhi, Mahatma, 92
Gestapu coup, 137
Goh Keng Swee, 70, 71
Golden Khersonese, 14
Greater India Society, 97
Greco-Roman, 7, 66, 100
Greece, 52
Guangdong, 116
Gulf of Siam, 59

Hakka, 12
Han dynasty, 122
Hapsburg, 106
Harrison, Brian, 13
Hebrew, 52, 66, 81

Hellenic, 16
Hertogh, Maria, 3
Hindu, 18, 20, 43, 44, 59, 80, 92, 94, 95, 114
Hindu-Buddhist, 16, 20, 26, 42
Hokkien, 12, 50
Hong Kong, 9, 102, 103, 115–117
Hong Kong University, ix
Hong merchants of Canton, 61
huaqiao, 3, 12
Huntington, Samuel, 140

Iberia, 46, 48, 52, 53
Iberian Peninsula, 53
India, xi, 12, 13, 16–18, 20, 21, 42–44, 46, 48, 51, 53, 58, 64, 68, 73, 79, 80, 89, 92, 94, 96–111, 114, 115, 121, 127, 135, 141, 154, 157
Indian Mutiny (India, 1857), 89
Indian Ocean, 4, 14, 26, 31, 42, 67, 68, 90, 91
Indian subcontinent, 4, 16, 45, 61, 140
Indic civilisation, xi, 3, 4, 7, 12, 16–23, 26, 28, 29, 33, 34, 42, 43, 45, 46, 48, 51, 58, 62, 63, 65, 66, 79, 80, 88, 92–94, 100, 114, 135, 141, 157, 167
Indic civilisational, 25, 97
Indo-Aryan, 16, 100
Indochina, 13, 15, 96, 127
Indo-European, 16, 52, 62, 64
Indonesia, 28, 73, 89, 110, 127, 135–137, 147
Industrial Revolution, 30, 89, 103, 104

Irrawaddy, 15, 29, 94
Islamic civilisation, xi, 18, 43, 46, 49, 69, 81, 88, 92, 96, 99, 100, 135, 167
Islamic Ottoman, 88
Islamic *Ummah*, 52, 99, 147

Japan, ix, x, 11, 12, 49, 55, 60, 103–105, 119, 127–129, 135, 148, 154, 166, 167
Java, 18–20, 23, 27–29, 36, 46, 60, 68, 79, 80, 91
Java War (Java, 1825), 99
Jesuit, 45, 98, 122
Jew, 81
Jews of Kaifeng, 82
Jinnah, Muhammad Ali, 93
Johor Empire, 29, 62, 99, 111
Johor River, 48
Jurchen, 44

Karimun, 36
Khitan, 44
Khmer, 15–17, 19, 20, 23, 43, 44, 96
Konfrontasi campaign, 137
Korea, 20, 49, 104, 105, 119, 166, 167
Kuala Lumpur, 3, 9
Kuomintang (KMT), 76

Language Families
    Austro-Asiatic, 15
    Austronesian, 15, 18, 43
    Sino-Tibetan, 15
Laos, 135, 139, 147
League of Nations, 109, 129
Lee Kuan Yew, 71

Leninist Russia, 144
Linyi, 19
literacy, 22, 32–34, 77
Louis XIV (French king), 58
Luzon, 23, 50

Macao, 50, 55, 61, 68, 98
Macartney, Lord George, 98
Macaulay, Thomas, 96
Maddison, Angus, 103
Madras, 91
Maharaj, Tilak, 92
mainland Southeast Asia, 15, 16, 18, 28, 42, 44, 45, 50, 52, 68, 70, 92, 94, 96
Majapahit Empire, 26, 79
Malabar Coast, 51, 55
Malacca, 12, 26, 48, 49, 60, 61, 68
Malacca Straits, 29, 89, 99
Malaya, 3, 11–13, 38, 52, 111, 127, 129, 135, 137
Malay Peninsula, x, 9, 13, 14, 19, 24, 28, 50, 91, 97
Malaysia, 9, 71, 89, 137, 147
Mallet du Pan, Jacques, 68
Maluku Spice Islands, 48, 53, 55, 60, 61
Manichaeism, 81
Manila Galleon trade, 50
Manipur, 97
Mao Zedong, 131, 138, 142
Maratha, 95
maritime Southeast Asia, 91, 154
May 13 Riots (Kuala Lumpur, 1969), 3

May Fourth generation, 105
May Fourth Movement, 75
Mediterranean, 4, 7, 12, 14, 17, 31, 42, 45, 48, 50–56, 62, 90, 98, 100
Meiji Japan, 104, 167
Meiji Restoration, 70
Mekong, 15, 16, 29, 94
Menam Chao Phraya, 15, 16, 29, 94
merantau, ix, x, 10, 11, 27, 72, 73, 111, 117, 126, 140
Mexico, 50
Middle East, 82, 135, 140, 144
Mill, James, 96
Minangkabau, 10, 26, 99, 113
Ming authorities, 50
Ming dynasty, 26, 49, 50, 58, 82, 101, 122
Minto, Lord Gilbert, 68, 91
modern civilisation, xi, 3, 4, 6–9, 11, 25, 26, 31, 34, 37, 38, 48, 55, 58, 62, 65–68, 72, 88–90, 92, 104, 128, 140, 144, 157, 167
Modi, Narendra, 114
Mon, 15, 16, 23, 43, 45, 50
Mongol, 26, 36, 44, 48, 49, 101, 102, 122
Mon-Khmer, 18
Mughal, 58, 64, 88, 89, 92, 95
Muslim, 7, 31, 46, 48–50, 53, 55, 60, 95, 96, 98, 102, 116
Muslim Sepoy revolt (Singapore, 1915), 97
mutually assured destruction (MAD), 131

Nalanda Project, 114
Nanhai trade, 20
Nanyang, 3, 12
Narai (King of Ayutthaya Kingdom), 45
nation, ix, 2–5, 36–38, 66–68, 74, 81, 88, 90, 103, 105, 106, 117, 128, 129, 134, 136, 144, 147, 152, 154, 155, 162, 166
national culture, 3, 4, 6, 9, 23, 34, 38, 39, 66, 69, 127, 129, 133, 146, 149, 150, 153, 156, 167
national empire, 6, 7, 26, 37, 38, 68, 72, 128, 133, 140, 146, 163
National Socialism in Germany, 108
nation-states, 7, 23, 37, 89, 101, 102, 105, 106, 108, 109, 111, 112, 114, 119, 123, 126–133, 136, 137, 140, 142–144, 146–149, 152, 160, 162, 163, 166, 167
Needham, Joseph, 78
Nehru, Jawaharlal, 93
Nepal, 91
Nile, 52, 79
Nixon, Richard, 138
Non-Aligned Movement, 136
North Atlantic Treaty Organisation (NATO), 134–136, 142, 148
Nusantara, 12, 15, 18, 20, 21, 23, 25–27, 46, 50, 60, 61, 79, 80, 91, 92, 97, 99, 111, 115, 140

Opium Wars, 88, 98
Orang Asli, 154

Orang Laut, 154
Ottoman caliphate, 97, 98
Ottoman Empire, 57
Ottoman Turks, 48

Pacific Ocean, 50, 100
Padri movement, 98, 113
Pan-Asianism, 97
Parsees, 81
Parti Kommunis (PKI), 137
Penang, 68, 72
People's Republic of China (PRC), 130, 131, 141, 142, 144, 146–149, 153
Perak, 12
Persia, 26, 52, 82
Persian Gulf, 23, 26, 43, 48, 98
Philippines, 18, 24, 55, 110, 127, 133, 135, 136
pluralism, 29, 30
Portugal, 46, 52, 53, 107
Portuguese, 45
post-Renaissance Europe, 55
Prambanan, 80
progress, 11, 31, 32, 35, 36, 63, 65, 86, 87, 89, 105, 120, 121, 129, 133, 164
Protestant, 30, 56, 57, 64, 65
Putin, Vladimir, 163
Pyu-Myanmar, 44

Qianlong (Emperor of the Qing dynasty), 68, 98
Qin Gang, 153

Qing dynasty, 82, 88, 92, 96–98, 100–103, 115, 116, 167
Qing Manchu, 58
Qin-Han Empire, 166

Raffles, Stamford, 36, 68, 71, 73, 91, 115
Rajput, 95
Rama IV, 96
Rama V, 96
Red River valley, 15
Red Sea, 23, 43, 48
Reformation, 30, 57, 60
Reid, Anthony, 45
Renaissance Europe, 30, 57
Republic of China (ROC), 103, 131, 142, 144, 153, 167
Riau-Lingga Archipelago, 29, 48
Roman Empire, 53
Roosevelt, Theodore, 129
Roy, Ram Mohan, 92
Russia, 100, 108, 142, 163
Russian, 101, 142
Russian Revolution (1917), 110

Salween, 15, 16, 29
Sanskrit, 33, 63
scientific revolution, 65
Semitic, 17, 52
Shan, 45
Showa (emperor of Japan), 12
Siam, 12, 26, 59, 92, 96
Siege of Peking, 103

Singapore, ix, 2, 3, 5, 7–9, 11, 13, 25, 26, 29, 30, 34, 36, 38, 48, 52, 62, 67, 68, 70–74, 76, 91, 97, 111, 115–117, 126, 127, 135, 137, 139, 147–149, 151, 155–157, 159, 160, 166
Singaporean, 158
Sinic civilisation, xi, 4, 6, 8, 20, 23, 34, 43, 44, 48, 49, 58, 63–66, 79–81, 96, 97, 101, 103–105, 118–120, 141, 143, 147, 149, 166, 167
Sino-Thai, 159, 160
socialism, 3, 76, 110, 144
Song dynasty, 122
South Africa, 91
South Asia, 114
South China Sea, 4, 14, 15, 19–21, 26, 49, 72, 144, 146, 152, 153
    nine-dash line, 153
Southeast Asia, xi, xii, 3–5, 7, 11, 13, 19–21, 24, 27, 32–35, 38, 43, 46, 52, 59, 69, 83, 91, 96, 98, 101, 107, 110, 111, 113, 114, 119, 126, 127, 132, 133, 135, 136, 140, 147, 148, 152, 159, 161
Southeast Asia Treaty Organisation (SEATO), 136, 137
Soviet Union, 7, 11, 76, 128, 130, 131, 136, 138, 142, 143, 148
Spain, 46, 52, 53, 107
Sri Vijaya, 20, 21, 23, 26, 29, 33, 79, 80
Straits Settlements, 12, 97, 111
Sufi, 46, 99
Sukarno, 137
Sulawesi, 26, 29

Sulu Sea, 23
Sumatra, 26, 28, 33, 46, 61, 80, 91, 98
Sun Yat-sen, 102, 116
Suvarnabhumi, 14
swaraj movement, 97

Tagore, Rabindranath, 93
Tai, 45
Taiwan, 18, 60, 144–146
Tang dynasty, 22, 82, 121, 122
Taoism, 80
technology, 35, 75, 78, 79, 108, 120, 129, 164
Tiananmen, 143
Tibet, 43, 91, 102
Tigris-Euphrates, 52, 79
Timor Leste, 34, 159
Tokugawa Japan, 92, 101
Tongking, 97
Toynbee, Arnold, 77
Treaty of Nanking, 102, 115
Treaty of Westphalia, 106
Tsarist Russian, 106
Turko-Mongol, 26, 43

Ujong Tanah, x, 9, 11, 13, 27, 52, 126
Undang-Undang Laut Melaka, 47
United Nations (UN), 129–131, 134, 135, 142, 147, 163
United States (US), 7, 11, 37, 67, 100, 106, 127, 129–131, 136–138, 140–148, 151, 153, 154, 161
UN Security Council, 129, 130

UN Sustainable Development
   Goals, 157

Viet, 15, 16
Vietnam, 19, 20, 43, 79, 92, 97, 98,
   104, 105, 110, 119, 131, 135, 137,
   147, 166, 167
Vietnam War, 137, 138

Wahhabism, 98
Warsaw Pact, 134
Western Europe, 5, 56, 62, 64, 66,
   129, 131
Wilson, Woodrow, 129
World War I, 97, 108, 111, 129
World War II, x, 4, 7, 8, 109, 111,
   126, 128

Xuantong, 103

Yangtze River, 15, 78
Yellow River, 78
Yi Jing, 21
Yuan dynasty, 101
Yuan Shikai, 103
Yue, 15

zhongguo wenhua (中国文化), 119,
   149, 166
zhonghua wenming (中华文明), 119,
   149, 166
Zheng He, 26, 49
Zhenla, 16
Zhou dynasty, 101
Zoroastrianism, 81

www.ingramcontent.com/pod-product-compliance
Lightning Source LLC
Chambersburg PA
CBHW061939220426
43662CB00012B/1966